PUBLIC ORDER CRIMINAL BEHAVIOR AND CRIMINAL LAWS: THE QUESTION OF LEGAL DECRIMINALIZATION

KENNETH A. JOHNSON

San Francisco, California
1977

Published by

R & E RESEARCH ASSOCIATES, INC.
4843 Mission Street
San Francisco, California 94112

Publishers
Robert D. Reed and Adam S. Eterovich

Library of Congress Card Catalog Number

76-56560

I.S.B.N.
0-88247-441-3

ACKNOWLEDGEMENTS

Over the time period entailed in completing my study the manuscript benefitted substantially from the comments and suggestions of numerous individuals. Special appreciation is extended to Dr. Victor Gecas and especially Dr. Steven Burkett who provided valuable and constructive criticisms and helped clarify some of the basic ideas in the work. I am deeply grateful to Dr. Louis Gray who contributed helpful suggestions and without whose friendship and encouragement I might not have persevered. I wish to acknowledge my appreciation to several friends who helped in the initial stages of the research. Statistical analysis was facilitated through the assistance of Dr. John Carlson in setting up the computer program; and data collection was attributable to the endeavors of John Karlson, without whose efforts the study would not have been possible. I am also indebted to the typist, Mrs. Anna Conditt, for the care and invaluable skill she gave to the typing of the manuscript. Finally, I wish to express my gratitude to my family for their love, encouragement and support throughout the course of the research.

TABLE OF CONTENTS

APPENDIX

LIST OF TABLES

CHAPTER 1

INTRODUCTION

Statement of the Problem

The purpose of the present study is to test and evaluate certain basic postulations of the labeling perspective of social deviance.[1] Reactivated in the fifties by Lemert (1951) and expanded by Becker (1963), the perspective has increasingly become of interest recently in efforts toward the generation of more contingent theoretical explanations in the study of deviant behavior.

Research and theoretical emphasis in the labeling orientation has been largely on the "process" of becoming deviant and the part played by the official registrars of deviation (e.g., police, courts, correction agencies, etc.) in that process (Matza, 1969). Put in another way, this process is called "social reaction." As Kitsuse (1962:347) interprets it:

> Clearly, the forms of behavior per se do not activate the processes of societal reaction which sociologically differentiate deviants from non-deviants. Thus a central problem for theory and research in the sociology of deviance may be stated . . . What are the behaviors which are defined as deviant, and how do these definitions organize and activate the societal reaction by which persons come to be differentiated and treated as deviant?

Similarly, Becker (1963:9) has observed that "deviance is not a quality of the act the person commits, but rather a consequence of the application by others of rules and sanctions to an offender." Therefore deviance is viewed as a consequence of the responses of others to a person's act. This perspective has subsequently become a major position of the social interactionist and labeling approach to the study of deviance (Erikson, 1962; Schur, 1965; Goffman, 1969; Matza, 1969). Numerous studies have since augmented and expanded on this theme (e.g., Wilkins, 1965; Skolnick, 1966; Scheff, 1966; Circourel, 1969; and Wiseman, 1970).

Relatively few empirical studies have been forthcoming, however, that specifically elucidate or give credence and support to "labeling" theoretical propositions. Thus, labeling views can be said to be "long on theory and short on empirical evidence" (Gibbons, 1973:206). More to the point, and consistent with the aims of the present research, the labeling perspective is in need of systematic elimination of certain glaring ambiguities in its theoretical infrastructure before it can lay claim to full stature as "theory" in sociology. As it now stands, the labeling orientation toward deviance remains a set of plausible contentions about deviance rather than a well documented collection of empirical generalizations (Schur, 1971).

The labeling approach nevertheless takes up much of the slack either ignored or omitted in other theoretical treatments of deviant behavior. A central conduit in the explanation of deviance, according to labeling theorists, is the diverse part played by society and social values in defining the nature of criminal behavior. This includes society's role in identifying criminals, in selecting those that will be punished, and in deciding the severity of that punishment. As a result, the labeling approach encompasses processes through which the criminal becomes legally defined as well; or with the genesis of the criminal law. In the "new" perspective in deviance a great deal of emphasis is being placed upon societal reaction in the establishment of legal statutes creating deviants (Becker, 1963).[2]

The sociological analysis of the criminal law stresses the nature of law as a dynamic reality generated in a social crucible as opposed to something that develops according to its own internal logic without regard for other social processes.[3] Of critical importance in this view is the influence of the special interest group on changes in the criminal law, or in the social role of law.[4] The formulation and administration of law is being viewed from within the interest structure of politically organized society (Quinney, 1969; 20-30; see also Tannebaum, 1938; Jeffery, 1959; Turk, 1969; Gibbs, 1966; Chambliss, 1969; and Hills, 1971). Consequently, research on labeling theory may be more appropriately tested by addressing itself to the prevailing social attitudes or social reactions that define criminal behavior, both legal and moral.

The labeling approach focuses on the reaction of a social audience to a particular kind of behavior. This reaction is reflected in a social label, social designation or stereotype imputed to a person on the basis of some information about him (Payne, 1973). Public reactions toward types of deviant behavior do not necessarily remain constant but over a period of time may change in response to new social conditions, social norms and scientific knowledge. "Behavior that is defined as criminal today may be reevaluated as 'sick,' viewed as legitimate, or even positively valued" (Hills, 1971:61-63). Disapproved deviations, however, may encounter various degrees of sanction, varying all the way from a certain amount of tolerance to mild and even strong disapproval (Clinard, 1974). Thus, rules or laws that have been created and maintained by the labeling of that behavior as deviant are not universally agreed upon (Becker, 1963).[5] Public order or "victimless" crimes such as abortion,[6] prostitution, homosexuality, and the use of narcotics, exemplify types of behavior toward which enactment of criminal laws is most controversial. Yet we know very little about public attitudes toward these laws or whether public sentiments and perspective in relation to them have experienced change over time.

The present study therefore attempts to explore public attitudes toward crime and criminal laws and, more specifically, to test "social reaction" hypotheses derived from the labeling literature by examining the extent of support shown for policies dealing with public order crimes and criminals in a non-metropolitan community.[7] Studies involving more urban populations[8] have recently been the object of considerable attention which has sometimes been national in scope and focus.[9] These studies, however, appear bereft of theoretical considerations, either in the design of the research or in corollary modes of analysis and explanation in research findings. This research investigation will hopefully permeate some of the vacuum existing between the fact of data collection and that of theory construction in the study of social deviance in general and labeling in particular.

Briefly stated in recapitulation, the purpose of the present study can be said to focus on the following concerns within a labeling frame of reference: (1)

the selection process by which various acts are labeled criminal and various individuals singled out as criminals to be punished; and (2) the nature of the relationship between extant public order criminal laws and policies and public toleration for modification or decriminalization of such laws.

Public Order Crime and Criminal Laws

Public order crimes are a subclass within the broad category of social deviance and refer to the assignment or labeling of deviants whose crimes do not injure others. Schur (1965:12) defines them as "the attempt to control, by criminal law, the willing exchange of socially disapproved but widely in demand goods . . . ." Abortion, prostitution, homosexuality and drug addiction are examples of the types of public order crimes under investigation in the present study.[10]

Clinard and Quinney (1973) have constructed a typology of criminal behavior systems in which they delineate categories of legal aspects of public order criminal behavior and societal reactions to them (Table 1.1). The authors stress that public responses to such crimes are not disturbing to all community members. Many of the crimes are considered "victimless" in that only willing participants are involved. While there is no victim in the sense of a complainant, some members of the community feel threatened by these behaviors. In many cases the community also feels it is protecting the person against themselves.

Much of what is called crime in American criminal law has been formulated for the purpose of publicly enforcing moral principles (Quinney, 1970). Since the conduct in question is not injurious to other persons or property, it can be considered as an attempt by society to regulate the kinds of behavior that disturbs its sense of public morality.

The application of criminal law does not operate in a vacuum. There exists in a very real sense an interdependence of the criminal justice system with society's norms and mores. As Cohen and Short (1971) have stated:

The impact of the law upon behavior depends on the moral

4

status of the law . . . the extent to which the rules of the legal system agree or disagree with the values and norms of the people to whom these rules apply, and the respect and legitimacy that are attributed to the police, the courts, and other agencies of the institutions of justice (1971:95).

Cohen and Short further note that:

> There are laws whose necessity is universally conceded; and there are others that are supported by some part of the public and denounced as intolerable infringements of the liberty or privacy by others. Even with respect to the same crimes, attitudes may vary from general consensus to bitter consensus (1971:95).

Such has been the case with public order crimes. That is, public responses toward them have been differential in nature. Although these types of crimes may be without a victim, they are nevertheless disturbing to many community members. There is strong reaction to public order offenders by some segments of society and weak reactions by others.

Goldman (1970) views such laws as "indicators" of the breakdown of society. Social deviance is considered problematic because of the reaction of members of the society to strain in the social system (social disequilibrium produced by non-conforming members). Thus, high deviancy rates, according to Goldman, serve as systemic warnings to a society that many needs of large segments of the population are not met. Moreover, because there are few complainants, laws regulating public crimes are virtually unenforceable. Only a small portion of the offenses result in either detection or arrest.

TABLE 1.1.

TYPOLOGY OF CRIMINAL BEHAVIOR SYSTEMS

Category	Public Order Criminal Behavior
Legal Aspects of Selected Offenses	Specific criminal laws embody the moral sense of particular segments of the community. Such offenses as prostitution, homosexuality, drunkenness, and drug use are disturbing to some community members. Many of the crimes are "victimless" in

| | that only willing participants are involved. Yet it is easier for the power elite to outlaw these behaviors than to either accept them or to change the social arrangements that produced the behaviors. |
| Social Reaction and Legal Processing | Strong reaction by some segments of society, weak reaction by others. Only a small portion of the offenses result in arrest. Sentences are strong for some offenses, such as the possession of narcotic drugs. |

SOURCE: Clinard and Quinney, 1973:18.

The Question of Legal Decriminalization

The problem of public order crimes has recently become so difficult that there is serious discussion of eliminating or "decriminalizing" them from criminal codes on the grounds that these crimes constitute an "overreach of the criminal law" (see Clinard and Quinney, 1973; Mannheim, 1946; Allen, 1964; Kadish, 1967; Jeffery, 1970; Sykes, 1972; Wilkins, 1973; and Motley, 1973).

Among some major consequences of this overreach of the criminal law have been the overburdening of the legal system of enforcement and judicial administration, the impairment of its effectiveness to contend with more serious crime problems, and the fostering and sustaining of various kinds of crime. Decriminalization adherents regard negative public sentiments toward public order criminals as largely due to present wholesale stigmatization by the law, and therefore likely to change with changes in the law. Proponents of this point of view persist in the assertion that public order crimes should be reviewed for immediate removal from the criminal law and placed within a treatment system.[11]

In counter arguments generally advanced by advocates for the continuance of legal statutes on public order crime, it is maintained that public order acts project consequences for the society as a whole. Geis (1972:4), for example, perceives legal decriminalization of public order crimes as problematic. Society is seen to suffer from transgressions against norms that are formalized into criminal statutes. Public order criminal behavior serves to weaken social values, and norms, and may provide undesirable models of behavior. Gusfield (1967) and Hills (1971:8) reiterate the "symbolic function" of public order criminal laws over the more instrumental social control functions of such laws. Symbolic functions do not depend necessarily on the successful enforcement of the law for their effect; rather the mere existence of the laws symbolize the public affirmation and dominance of certain social ideals and norms at the expense of others.

Schwartz and Orleans (1967:543) subject to empirical examination some widely held assumptions regarding the operation and effectiveness of legal sanctions (in this case sanctions concerning compliance with payment of federal income taxes) and found that cultural attitudes and social structural factors correlate with legal sanctions. Legal sanctions, or the threat of sanctions, combine with normative orientations and are capable of "inducing morality." All the above perspectives argue that public order criminal acts not only break the criminal law but also do harm to the larger society by breaking its cohesiveness and by damaging its "moral fiber" (Geis, 1972). The moot nature of the question of legal decriminalization of public order crimes is thus evident.

Today the moral acceptance of abortion,[12] marijuana use, narcotics, and homosexuality are being publicly discussed and movements championing them have recently emerged (Gusfield, 1967).[13] A relationship between legal development and social change may well exist.[14] Because collective activity on the part of deviant minorities is currently on the upswing in the country, both through legitimate organizations and the mass media, the question may be asked: what is the nature of public reaction to such phenomena? In research on the "criminalization of deviance" the substantive nature of these reactions receive a good deal of attention; that is, how and why the public reacts to particular "offenses" as they do (Schur, 1965). As Turk (1966:341) states: "the problem of relating (social reaction) and crime is one accounting for the assignment of criminal statutes, which means that actual offensive behavior is treated not as the phenomena to be explained, but instead as one of a number of variables related to the <u>probability of criminalization</u>" (emphasis added). The present study will attempt to determine, as one major dimension, the magnitude of public reaction and toleration for modification of public order criminal laws.

Public Policy Implications

The assessment of deviance theory for public policy implications is a second approach within a criminalization of deviance context. This entails the possibility that sociologists may have direct interest in contributing to the formulation of criminal laws. As one legal expert has stated: "the question, what sorts of behavior should be declared criminal (i.e., legal criminalization or decriminalization), is one to which the behavioral sciences (and sociology in particular) might contribute vital insights . . ." (Schur, 1965:5; 1968). When viewed sociologically, laws are always an outcome of social processes. Sociological research may thus serve to guide public policy with respect to most behaviors defined as criminal and most public reactions to those behaviors.

Against the background of current views on public order criminal policy reviewed in Chapter One in this paper, the second chapter presents the review of existing literature on labeling theory and Chapters Three and Four provide the research design and methodology for analysis and synthesis of public reactions to public order criminal laws and criminals. Chapter Five is an analysis of the data and Chapter Six discusses the application and integration of research findings on labeling theory.

CHAPTER 2

REVIEW OF LITERATURE

Two major trends characterize the development of the labeling approach over the past fifty years: (1) emphasis on social control processes in the defining of persons as criminal, involving social control agencies (e.g., police, courts, etc.) and (2) theoretical work on the definition and perpetuation of deviance under the heading of the societal reaction to deviance (Bordua, 1967). The latter position is the focus of the present study. Social reaction is an integral component in the social process by which certain types of behavior come to be defined as criminal and whereby individuals are selected out for deviant status.[15] The current popularity of the social reaction hypothesis in recently published works in the field of deviance and the potential utility of the concept as a central research variable in the present work suggest that it would be useful to review how it has been used in the literature on labeling theory.

Theoretical Works

Societal reaction to crime as a concept in American sociology first developed as an explanation for the emergence of delinquent gangs (Thrasher, 1926) and the progressive social separation and consequent cultural and group differentiation of criminals because of arrest and stigma (Sutherland, 1938). Sellin (1938) epitomized the relativity of public definitions of crime as value conflict and the role of stigmatization in generating criminal careers.

Further refinement and elaboration of labeling effects on criminal careers evolved from sociological theoreticians such as Tannebaum (1938), Lemert (1951), Becker (1963), and Erikson (1962; 1966). Tannebaum (1938) considered the specialized treatment of the apprehended juvenile delinquent as a "dramatization of evil" and contended that this process played a greater role in making the criminal than perhaps any other experience. Lemert (1951) developed the concept of "societal

9

reaction" as a major ingredient in what he referred to as "secondary deviation."
Development of criminal careers is primarily contingent upon the nature of societal
response to deviation and the subsequent perception and internalization of this
public "image" on the part of the deviant. Lemert (1951:22) writes:

> . . . persons and groups are differentiated in various ways,
> some of which results in social penalties, rejection, and segre-
> gation. These penalties and segregative reactions of society of
> the community are dynamic factors which increase, decrease, and
> condition the form which the initial differentiation or deviation
> takes . . . . The deviant person is one whose role, status,
> function and self-definition are importantly shaped by how much
> deviation he engages in, by the degree of its social visibility,
> by the particular exposure he has to the societal reaction, and
> by the nature and strength of the societal reaction.

Becker (1963) reactivated Lemert's secondary deviation and extended it to include the
rule-making (i.e., laws) or political processes whereby legal definitions of behavior
as criminal are extended. These processes he called "moral entrepreneurship," and
his principle examples were the promotion of laws against the use of marijuana and
opiates (Glaser, 1971:31). Erikson (1966) widened the application of relative definitions of deviance by illustrating how historical "Wayward Puritans" functioned to
stabilize boundaries of community toleration limits toward deviance.

The labeling perspective has recently been extended to include diverse and
far-ranging applications of "societal reaction" hypotheses. Among the topics considered have been mental illness (Scheff, 1959; Taber, et al., 1969); juvenile delinquency (Platt, 1969; Eisner, 1969; Faust, 1973; and Johnson and Grieneeks, 1973);
social problems (Rubington and Weinberg, 1968); alcoholism (Truce and Roman, 1970);
premarital sex (Reiss, 1970; law (Schur, 1968); the ex-felon (Stebbings, 1971); and
deviant ethnic minorities (Bustamante, 1972). Only the more pertinent of these works
will be discussed below.

Scheff (1966:34) uses Becker's distinction between rule-breaking behavior
which is a property of the act, and deviance, which is a property of the reaction of
others to the act. Scheff calls deviance that is recognized and labeled by others

"residual deviance" and believes this to be a better term for mental illness. Taber,

et al. (1969) compare five definitions of mental illness and conclude that social

judgements of behavior are evident in all five. As will later be seen, the above

theoretical perspectives, especially those of Scheff, function as a major axis for

empirical research and conceptual clarification on the issue of mental illness as

deviation.

Eisner (1969) concentrates on official records and other definitional cri-

teria (society acting corporately through its designated authorities) that result in

the assignment of the "delinquency" label. Faust (1973) further delineates the con-

sequences of a delinquent label to the self-esteem of the deviant. Quinney (1970b)

illuminates the "social reality" of social reaction to crime, making distinctions

between legal and extralegal reactions and sanctions. Quinney (1970b:278) states:

> Social reactions are normatively patterned according to such
> contingencies as the type of offense, the personal and social
> characteristics of the offender, the social location of the
> offense, and the degree to which the offense violates other social
> norms. All these affect the manner and regularity with which re-
> actions (both legal and extralegal) will be practiced. Social
> reactions, like all other forms of behavior, are to be understood
> according to their social patterning and cultural regulation.

Quinney's distinction between some facet of the "culture" of a society and the "social

organization" of a society is invaluable for purposes of the present research. This

approach entails an analysis of legal norms in relation to their underlying values and

to the social units or status groupings that are the object of legal norms. "With the

aid of this approach it would in principle appear possible to discover how legal norms

are reinterpreted and transformed over time" (Evans, 1962:5).

These theoretical assumptions[16] held by labeling theories were rarely sub-

jected to empirical testing or verification prior to 1960. Since that time, however,

it is accurate to say that there has been a rapid growth of interest in empirical

studies on labeling, particularly of the societal reaction premise.

11

Empirical Studies

Empirical studies on labeling theory can be divided into two major categories: (1) studies dealing with the social origins of stigmatic labels or on the process of defining persons and behaviors as criminal; and (2) studies that assess the social-psychological consequences of the labeling process on self-conceptions and self-esteem of deviants and on the development and perpetuation of deviant careers (e.g., Gould, 1969; Jensen, 1972; William and Weinberg, 1970; Foster, et al., 1972; and Burkett, 1972). The former category is more directly related to theoretical issues of labeling theory addressed in the present study. In this category, labeling is taken as the dependent variable, and the search is for sociological variables that may causally influence the labeling process (Hagan, 1973b:447). This may include various "reactors" to criminally defined phenomena; from the community at large, various social institutions, or the agents of social control (e.g., Chiricos, et al., 1972; Marshall and Purdy, 1972; Rushing, 1971; and Linsky, 1970).

Social Reaction Hypotheses

We have noted that the reaction of a community to an act that results in a person's being labeled as a deviant is an important process in understanding the nature of deviant behavior. Stemming from Scheff (1966) and Taber's, et al. (1964) early labeling propositions on mental illness, a number of studies have since emanated from this perspective. Linsky (1970b:305), for example, tested the societal reaction model by investigating the relationship between a community's common culture and the incidence of hospitalization rates for mental disorders. Findings reveal that hospitalized mental illness is higher in culturally homogeneous communities because of greater consensus as to what constitutes normal or abnormal behavior, rather than because of societal reaction or rejection. In Linsky's view, explanations of mental illness based on differential community responses do not operate with regard to some forms of mental illness--for example, psychoses. This pattern appears to be consistent with the findings of other investigators (e.g., Gove, 1970).

Additional studies on labeling and mental illness, however, show a degree of greater support, indeed tend to reinforce certain labeling propositions. Rushing (1971), for example, extends labeling to "contingencies" of the societal reaction by adding independent variables such as individual resources of the mental patient. Using samples of twenty-one to sixty-four year old male hospital admissions in three state mental hospitals in Washington as a measure of societal reaction, Rushing found that data consistently support the hypothesis that a person's family, occupational-economic and community status appear to be significant contingencies, or social support, in the tendency to hospitalize. Community isolation and deficiencies in individual resources appear to be significant in coercive individual hospitalization. The relation between the degree of individual integration and societal reaction, however, is untested in the study.

A number of research examples in the labeling tradition focus on specific social "audiences" in testing single propositions in labeling theory. Within this context, the reactions of criminal court judges in Florida and their willingness to impose stigmatic labels were investigated by Chiricos, et al. (1972). The researchers tested the disposition of the judges toward 2,419 felony cases and found significant inconsistencies in the imposition of a "convict" label by criminal court judges. Defendants who were older, black, poorly educated, had a prior record, and were defended by court-appointed attorneys were among the most likely to be labeled. These findings, argue the authors, could have serious implications for the development of criminal identities and careers (Chiricos, et al., 1970:569).

In an interesting study along similar lines, Marshall and Purdy (1972) further augment the labeling research frame of reference in applying the labeling model to the crime of drinking and driving. A significant facet of this study was the operationalization and control of "seriousness" and "frequency" of the act of drinking and driving so that individual characteristics might be assessed independently of the degree of deviance. Two samples from four courts in Los Angeles, California were examined. The labeling proposition was affirmed in that conviction was found to be a function of membership in certain social categories, regardless of degree of deviance. A number of serious questions remain unanswered by the study. First, the time dimension is problematic because there is no way of knowing the point in the process where labeling occurs. Furthermore, the responses of judges and jurors in the process of labeling were not taken into consideration.

Social Reaction and Public Order Crimes

There have been few attempts to analyse the relationship between the social reaction component in labeling theory and public order type crime and criminal laws. The majority of studies concerned with public order crimes have been in the nature of public opinion polls.[17] Consistent with the theme of deviant behavior as social process several studies have focused attention on the responses of others to public order type deviants.

Gilbert (1958) compared public responses of college students, prison inmates and the general public toward 19 felony statutes of the criminal law and found the social science students more inclined to take a general treatment attitude toward non-violent deviant sexual behavior (e.g., homosexuality). Relatively severe ratings were given, however, for narcotic peddling by all three groups. Similarly, Pattison, et al. (1968) described historical changes in public attitudes on narcotic addiction in a content analysis of popular magazines. Rehabilitation and treatment of the drug addict was favored rather than a strictly punitive approach.

Gibbons (1969), in a study complementing Gilbert's (1958), interviewed 320 California residents and analysed their responses toward specific criminal laws[18] (e.g., marijuana, narcotics and homosexuality laws) and public sentiments about appropriate punishments for such crimes. He found that severe penalties for possession of marijuana are not supported by most citizens but with other types of offenses (e.g., embezzlement and antitrust violations) citizens were harsh while the law was lenient. These research results indicate some empirical support for the social reaction postulate in that variations in punitive sanctions mirror public sentiments. Most citizens perceived the drug and sex deviant as "sick" and recommended psychiatric treatment for these individuals. Interestingly, over 65 percent of respondents recommended probation for narcotic and drug abusers. Furthermore, studies on attitudes toward juvenile control (Lentz, 1966) and research on public perceptions of the juvenile court (Parker, 1970) serve to illustrate that penalties chosen by the layman are not as severe as sanctions imposed by law.

Poveda (1972) described social reaction in a small town to alleged youthful drug abuse (much of which was unfounded), as contributing to a 92 percent increase in the number of juvenile arrests. Kitsuse (1962) tested social reaction hypotheses on homosexual behavior. Using a non-random sample of over 700 college undergraduates he attempted to document what behavior forms are interpreted as deviant, the process of definition, and the reactions to the deviance. Study findings support a "process" perspective by which persons come to be defined as deviant by others. Kitsuse concludes (1962:255) ". . . the critical feature of the deviant-defining process is not the behavior of individuals who are defined as deviant, but rather the interpretation others make of their behaviors, whatever those behaviors may be."

In research that generated much of the framework for the present study, Rooney and Gibbons (1966) attempted to ascertain the extent of support for public order criminal laws in a sample of California middle class respondents. An attempt was also made to determine if relationships existed between various social correlates and variations in societal reactions to these laws. Questions were included which probed for misconceptions about the facts regarding public order criminal activities, such as the belief that drug addicts are unusually prone to sexual misconduct, etc. (Gibbons, 1972:402). Research results reveal a general consensus toward more liberalized abortion laws but respondents were less tolerant of proposed changes in laws and practices regarding homosexuality and least accepting of changes in the handling of drug addicts. Many respondents called for severe penalties for

drug addicts. Males were slightly more tolerant than females on all three forms of
deviant behavior.

Simmons (1965; 1969) was one of the first to explicitly research public
attitudes and stereotypes of deviants, including public order criminals. Simmons'
aim was to explore the labeling process and its consequences by modifying techniques
previously developed for studying attitudes toward racial and cultural minorities.
The Bogardus social distance scale is one such technique. Using this scale, Simmons
provides data from a research survey designed to assess the average social distance
in terms of tolerance toward various deviant groups. In general, he found agreement
between the existence of discernible stereotypes of deviants and the content of these
stereotypes (Simmons, 1965:229). There were stereotypic descriptions for homosexuals
and marijuana smokers, among others (Table 2.1); and there was clear consensus on
traits assigned such deviants (Shoemaker, 1973). The present study draws heavily
upon Simmons' work.

Evaluation of Studies on Labeling

In the last decade in particular, the labeling approach has been the object
of much criticism which seems to conclude that the approach cannot "explain" deviance
as originally claimed. In general, a number of areas have been assessed to be in
need of attention. These are deficiencies and weaknesses in: (1) conceptualization;
(2) operational indicators; and (3) empirically testable propositions. Gibbs (1966:
12), for example, questions whether the labeling perspective differentiates between a
"substantive theory" of deviant behavior and conceptual treatment of it. In Gibb's
view, three major questions remain unanswered by the labeling approach: (1) why does
the incidence of a particular act vary from one population to the next; (2) why do
some persons commit the act while others do not; and (3) why is the act in question
considered deviant and/or criminal in some societies but not in others? Labeling
theory, according to Gibbs, stands in need of clarification as to what "kind" of
social reaction identifies deviant acts as deviant. Reiss (1970) further suggests

16

TABLE 2.1.

AVERAGE SOCIAL DISTANCE TOWARD VARIOUS DEVIANT GROUPS

Groups (In Order of Increasing Intolerance)	Mean Social Distance (Range 1 to 7)
Intellectuals	2.0
Ex-mental Patients	2.9
Atheists	3.4
Ex-convicts	3.5
Gamblers	3.6
Beatniks	3.9
Alcoholics	4.0
Adulterers	4.1
Political Radicals	4.3
Marijuana Smokers	4.9
Prostitutes	5.0
Lesbians	5.2
Homosexuals	5.3

SOURCE: J. L. Simmons, Deviants. Berkeley: The Glendessary Press:33.

that labeling theory may be fundamentally wrong for some types of deviation, for example, sexual deviation. Furthermore, one writer contends that Becker (1963) has overstated the effects of labeling in his definitions of deviance:[19]

> In (Becker's) definition acts can be identified as deviant only in reference to the reaction to them through labeling by society and its agents of social control . . . . . What this definition does is to reject, expressly or tacitly, a normative definition of deviance, even if it is broad and relative in scope . . . . . An act would not, therefore, be deviant unless it is detected and there is a particular kind of reaction to it. . . (therefore) if a couple engaging in adultery are not discovered and reacted to, they would not be deviant (Clinard, 1974:25).

Gouldner (1968) criticizes the labeling perspective of partisan attachment to an "underdog"; almost to the point of accepting a "distorted" view of social reality. Akers (1968) adds the accusation that labeling theorists overindulge in social definitions; thus, while labeling may create deviance and often operates to increase the probability that certain stigmatized persons will commit further deviant acts, the label per se does not create the behavior in the first place (Lowry, 1974).[20]

Additional critiques[21] of labeling theory follow closely and complement those above: it represents an overemphasis on external coercion and an under-emphasis on choice and opportunity (Fisher, 1972:83); the label of deviance is applied to subcultures and an underclass of powerless groups in society to the neglect of more powerful political elites (Liazos, 1972); and the labeling approach fails to integrate its theoretical position with previous perspectives on deviance (Lowry, 1974). Need-less to say, in the current analysis efforts will be directed toward correcting some of the limitations that have been noted in previous studies.

Criticisms of the labeling approach, some empirical validation for the theory notwithstanding, are not without some rebuttal on the part of labeling pole-mics. Schur (1971), for example, in a book devoted entirely to the subject of labeling deviant behavior, responds to critics by reiterating the importance of social processes social meanings, and social reactions to an explanation of deviant behavior. "Social reaction processes," argues Schur (1971:16) "affect the nature, distribution, social meanings, and implications of (deviant) behavior." The relative nature of definitions of crime is stressed:

> What is made of an act socially--indeed, one could say its very 'reality'--is crucially dependent on, or constituted of, the diverse social constructions individuals and groups place upon it. Such effects will not be appreciated if one persists in believing that 'deviance' somehow has an objective reality apart from the socially organized conceptions that define it. Ironically, it is precisely because of such socially patterned conceptions that Gibbs can feel such certainty as to which acts are, and which acts are not, deviant (Schur, 1969b:315).

In view of the fact that the degree of empirical data from the proliferation of deviance studies and research are accumulating, we can expect in the near future more extensive formulations relative to the primacy of the "societal reaction" postu-late in the labeling approach. In the meantime, and perhaps by necessity, the per-ception and interpretation a "social audience" makes of social behavior, whatever those behaviors may be, continues to be a critical and problematic variable in labeling research.

CHAPTER 3

THEORY AND HYPOTHESES

Conceptual Framework

The "social reaction" hypothesis is proposed to have potential relevance to the decriminalization of various public order crimes. Two theoretical constructs, or conceptual components, form a part of the social reaction hypothesis and are subject to empirical verification. These are public consensus on: (1) contingency of knowledge, or knowledge in the perception of deviance; and (2) contingency of punishment, or the degree and imposition of criminal or punitive sanctions.

These two conceptual elements in societal reactions to lawbreaking represent public interpretation and evaluation of deviant acts and the designation of appropriate treatment directed toward its control. From this point of view, crime is socially defined. Public consensus on knowledge in deviance perception and the degree of punitive sanction assigned deviants together describe the societal definition of public order deviant behavior.[22] The value of a labeling analysis in explaining deviance is related to the degree of consensus on social definitions of deviance and the probability of criminalization.

Knowledge and Deviance Perception

In the labeling approach to the study of deviance mechanisms of stereotyping emerge as central components of the social processes by means of which deviance is created. Public conceptions appear to deeply govern the whole process of deviance perception (Klapp, 1962; Goffman, 1965; Lentz, 1966; Simmons, 1965, 1967; Morris, 1966; McIntyre, 1967; and Schur, 1971). Similarly, what others believe about criminals is affected by knowledge about crime and the perception of its meaning. Social responses of any kind hinge upon these two realities. As Quinney (1970b:279) relates:

> Persons differ greatly in their knowledge about the existence
> and substance of laws in the society. Reaction to all that is
> associated with crime initially rests upon knowledge about crime
> . . . . Likewise, perceptions of the crime phenomena underlies

19

any social reaction to crime. How a person perceives crime provides a framework for his own understanding of and subsequent reaction to crime.

Thus, a population's social reaction to crime both proceeds from and results in the diffusion of criminal conceptions. This may mean that public knowledge or assumptions of an individual's involvement in deviation "overwhelms" what other knowledge of him it may have. Becker (1963) refers to this as the "master" deviant status. The public's picture or "image" of the deviant is primarily determined by the belief that he has deviated.[23] The nature and distribution of knowledge about particular deviants is therefore crucial to understanding societal responses to crime.

Criminologists presumably suspect that the public has distorted perceptions of the deviant. Lemert (1951) early proferred the idea that societal definitions of the deviant might be only vaguely formulated or even contradictory and ambivalent. Societal definitions often consist of a definite folklore and mythology built up around the deviant in the society which rejects him; "an integral body of rationalizations which are employed to justify the rejections and penalties inflicted upon the deviant as a result of societal reaction . . . . These become deeply laden with emotions and meanings that serve to define the deviant's expected behavior in societal interaction" (Lemert, 1951:64).

The exaggeration and distortion of the facts of deviation on the part of public perception, according to Lemert, creates what he refers to as the "putative deviation":

> The putative deviation is that portion of the societal definition of the deviant which has no foundation in his objective behavior. Frequently these fallacious imputations are incorporated into myth and stereotype and mediate much of the formal treatment of the deviant . . . . One illustration is the common belief in our culture that the taking of narcotic drugs disposes people to sexual depravity and criminality-- beliefs for which there is little or no proof (Lemert, 1951: 55-56).

Schur (1965) strongly concurs in the assumption that public reaction to public order crime and existing criminal laws is at least partly based on vital misconceptions about the nature of deviant behavior. Thus, the real effects of opiates on the addict's behavior and physical condition, the relative safety of most hospital abortions, and the non-stereotypical behavior of many homosexuals--all key facts--have been insufficiently emphasized in popular discussions of these forms of deviance (1965:175). Social "images" of the deviant therefore shape the societal reaction that shapes the accuracy of societal knowledge about the behavior in question.

Social Science and Public Order Deviants

To what extent are social expectations or lay theories of public order criminal behavior congruent with various scientific stances? In cases of abortion, prostitution, homosexuality and narcotic addiction, as previously mentioned, public reaction and existing legislation are at least partly based on vital misconceptions about the nature of the deviant behavior. However, no adequate research has yet been completed on the validity of popular images of various kinds of public order crimes.[24] Social scientific information on public order criminals is thus utilized in the study as a framework from which social reaction to these type crimes can be evaluated.[25]

Abortion--Social facts on abortion reveal that women in the lower socio-economic range receive fewer therapeutic abortions; in the case of unwed mothers, they also receive fewer therapeutic abortions percentagewise; the lower socio-economic woman usually goes through the dangerous process of self-induced abortion (Schur, 1965). The majority of abortions that take place in the United States are usually performed on married women. Rossi (1967:85) has noted that it is "highly probable that one in every two or three married women may undergo an illegal abortion during the years between their thirteenth and fiftieth birthday." About 85 percent of these abortions were done by physicians. Estimates on the number of illegal abortions in the United States prior to the new wave of reform legislation in some states generally span a range from 200,000 to 1.2 million (Bell, 1971). The majority of these were not arrests nor convictions.

21

Prostitution--Social scientific information on prostitution and prostitutes indicate that no correlation obtains between a decline in prostitution and an increase in crime. "The prostitute does not 'drain off' (the male client's) anti-social impulses for very long; statistics show that when prostitution declines, crime does too" (Geis, 1972:175). The common belief that prostitutes hate men has also proven to be erroneous (Gebhard, 1969). Neither is there support for the view that suppression of prostitution results in a rise in violent rape.[26]

Homosexuality--Information on homosexuality is considered more controversial than other public order type deviance. Yet the preponderance of historical and cross-cultural materials strongly support theories stressing the social basis of homosexual activity (Geis, 1972). One of the most common misconceptions about homosexuals is that they are an easily identifiable group. In reality, there is a wide divergence among homosexuals (Julian, 1973). It is estimated that only about 10 percent of the homosexual population is readily identifiable in terms of the stereotype (Hooker, 1957, 1958, 1966). Recent evidence suggests that many homosexuals are middle class lawyers, doctors and bankers (Hoffman, 1968; Leznoff and Westley, 1956). Furthermore, the great majority of sex researchers hold that homosexuality is not a disease but is a deep-rooted sexual orientation. Because more and more people are now accepting this view, homosexuals are winning ground in their efforts to improve their lives and avoid public stigma (Schott, 1967). Yet because of the prevalence of public misconceptions regarding them, homosexuals are currently categorically excluded from both military service and many kinds of civilian employment and in the past have been barred from civil service employment (e.g., Williams and Weinberg, 1971; Hoffman, 1968).

Narcotics--Research on the public order crime of heroin use dissipates many myths that surround the issue.[27] Regular use of heroin was prescribed by licensed physicians at one time in the United States. When this was the practice, there were a great number of heroin users but no heroin problems (Lindesmith, 1965).[28] There was minimal addict related crime at that time and a vast army of unemployable users

22

did not exist; opiate users worked regular hours like the rest of the population (Ashley, 1972). Under regular opiate use an individual may live as long as others and the drugs do not appear to effect either intelligence or physical performance (Geis, 1972:131).[29] Intelligence tests on addicts while on and off drugs show no appreciable differences, nor do tests of their capacity for physical performance, no matter how many years they have been on drugs (Brown and Partington, 1942:175-179).[30] The results of a nationwide survey in 1971 covering 222 companies revealed extensive drug problems in business firms in the United States. Over 53 percent of the firms responding had discovered drug indulgence among employees, including a few instances of selling and use of heroin on the facilities (Geis, 1972:135). Moreover, there is no relationship between the use of marijuana and the commission of crime (U.S. Senate Committee on Labor and Public Welfare, 1971:5). These "facts" concerning public order criminal deviation delineate the parameters of the knowledge contingency as indices of a "belief" component in the societal reaction concept, which constitutes the major independent variable in the study.

Belief, however, is usually recognized by what people say and do (Nettler, 1974). Belief and dispositions to action complement social reaction no less than other forms of behavior. The "behavioral" component in social reaction as a sociological concept is therefore the degree to which a population is willing to accord punishment or punitive sanctions to deviants.[31] This is the punishment contingency.

Social Reaction as Punishment Contingency

Social reaction assumptions in the labeling approach presuppose the existence of a relationship between public perception of deviance and punitive sanctions directed at offenders. Punishment is an indication that negative labels of stigma are being applied (Payne, 1973). Durkheim (1966:41) referred to this process as "widespread repressive sanction", defined as condemnation by public opinion that punishes all violators of moral rules. The process designates the limits of permissible or tolerable behavior by society and historically has undergone change and variation. These variations in the punishment contingency are therefore subject to analysis and explanation. As one writer observes: ". . . the empirical test or criterion of how strongly people feel in a given area is the degree to which they are willing to impose punishments (Duster, 1970:86). Because some parts of a population are more punitive than others the punitive reaction reflects the segmental organization of society.

Lemert (1967:43) identified three forms of inconsistency in the application of punitive sanctions or stigmatic labels by society:

1. Inconsistency or disproportion between stigma or punishments and the deviant attributes or actions toward which they are directed.

2. Inconsistent applications of stigma or penalties to the same person at different times or places.

3. Inconsistent penalties or stigma applied to persons in the same jurisdiction by the same law officials.

The present research is concerned with the first form of inconsistency described above as a measure of social reactions to legal decriminalization of public order crimes. The punishment contingency therefore focuses on treatment differentials, or degrees of punishment accorded the deviant in a community's response to deviance. If the respondent defines an individual's behavior as deviant, that is, agrees with legally designated statutes or criminalization, but does not accord him differential or punitive treatment as a consequence of that definition, then the individual is not sociologically deviant. Thus, a community should recommend treatment of deviants in accordance with the community's diagnosis of why he is that way.

Consensus and continuity in public perception of deviance should consequently occur. Respondents who are intolerant toward one deviant group should tend to be intolerant toward other deviant groups. Conversely, tolerance for one deviant group should result in greater overall tolerance for legal decriminalization of deviant groups in the study. This expected perception-clustering we may call the "deviance-perception crystallization" hypothesis (DPC). The major thematic focus of the research can be summarized as involving two dependent variables: (1) community consensus on

24

legal decriminalization, or modification of public order criminal laws by their removal from legal statutes; (2) community consensus on various treatment modalities which may be either punitive or non-punitive. A major independent variable is deviance perception and its relationship to both legal decriminalization and punitive sanction.

Social Correlates of the Societal Reaction:
Defining Independent Variables

Social correlates of tolerance for legal decriminalization of public order crimes comprise the remaining content of the present study. Social correlates, all independent variables, are hypothesized to influence societal reactions to the dependent variables criminal laws and punishment. These are: (1) community size; (2) socio-economic status; (3) sex differentials; (4) religious affiliation; and (5) age. Variations in these social background factors complement social reactions as reflecting the segmental organization of society. Because social reactions vary considerably from one segment to another and are not generalized for the entire society, social correlates are presumed to affect both the knowledge gradient in deviance perception and punitive sanction and also the degree levels in tolerance toward modification of criminal laws.

The first social correlate hypothesis, community size, predicates the existence of gradations in the structure of human aggregates (see especially, Clinard, 1964, 1968; Fischer, 1971). Previous sociological studies have utilized the rural-urban continuum as a basis for distinguishing between groups that are different from one another in attitudes, tastes, or behavior.[32] Rural-urban comparisons have often proven significant in the study of fertility rates, family behavior, religious and recreational activities, organizational participation, and other aspects of social life. Rural and urban communities also usually have different kinds of social problems (Geist and Fava, 1964:40). U.S. Bureau of the Census demographic delineations have made the definitions of urban and rural community a more valid and useful reflection of community patterns. These definitions form the basis for the determination of community size and rural and urban regions in the present study.[33]

In general, community size is expected to relate to tolerance for legal decriminalization of public order crimes independently of other co-variant factors. City dwellers should be more tolerant than their otherwise identical counterparts in less urban areas (Fischer, 1971). Persons from rural areas have also been found to assign harsher punishments for crimes which generally occur more frequently in the urban areas (Rose and Prell, 1955; Wilkins, 1964). The range of permitted sexual behavior also changes as city size decreases (Chapman, 1968). Ruralism, as opposed to urbanism, represents a cherished life style that some people seek to preserve within small towns in all regions of the country (Feldman and Thieban, 1972).

If community size reflects tolerance for certain forms of deviation, then a proportional increase in tolerance should be evident as one proceeds from the small community to the larger metropolis. Within this context, it is hypothesized that: the more urban a person's place of residence, the more likely he is to be tolerant toward legal decriminalization of public order crimes.

The second hypothesis is based on the variable of socio-economic status (SES). The socio-economic position of the person has been shown to affect his chances for education, income, occupation, and even life expectancy. Social class or status is, furthermore, one of the most important variables in social research and has had wide application in studies of juvenile delinquency, the family, attitudes toward stealing, unemployment compensation laws, gambling, and the control of crime (e.g., Nye, 1958; Gluecks, 1962; Hirschi, 1969; Smigel, 1956; Newman, 1957; Gardiner, 1967; McIntyre, 1967). Previous sociological studies by Rooney and Gibbons (1966) and others (e.g., Lentz, 1966) have also shown that socio-economic status is related to greater knowledge and to a decline of beliefs in certain misconceptions of deviants which were unfounded in fact. Higher SES persons were more consistent in their thinking, more likely to deemphasize punishment, and place greater emphasis on professional assistance for deviants. The social status of respondents in the present research, consequently, should have noticeable impact upon tolerance levels for modifications in

26

criminal laws involving victimless crimes: the higher the socio-economic status levels of respondents, the greater will be the tolerance for legal decriminalization of public order crimes.

Sex differentials and age are selected as the third and fourth independent variables. Females have traditionally been associated with more conservative values. This fact has been clearly explicated in the literature and research on sex-role socialization in American society (e.g., Parsons, 1942; Andreas, 1971). Females are thus socialized to accept their feminine identity, which includes submissiveness and acquiescence to conventional norms. Educational institutions, furthermore, tend to teach deference and maintenance to the social order and to train individuals to fit positions in the social order based on sex-roles. Agencies of social control and even institutions such as religion, the mass media and popular literature all stipulate the proper behavior of men and women, and it is the women who are expected to be more conforming, less independent and more "tradition-bound" in their role values and expression than the male. The liberation of women (a more recent phenomenon) on the other hand, has resulted in a deemphasis of conventionality and has been shown to accompany industrialization and urbanism (Reisman, 1959). In the present study we would therefore anticipate that: males will demonstrate more positive attitudes toward legal decriminalization of public order crimes than will females. This should hold constant even when age is considered in the analysis.

Chronological age is thought to be associated with public dispositions toward reform in public order criminal laws. Older persons have been described in social research as being more accepting of the status-quo, for numerous reasons; they also average less schooling than those who are younger. Each age group in our society has had on the average more formal education than the next older group (Burgess, 1962). Past studies reveal that less educated persons are more intolerant to changes in criminal laws (Rooney and Gibbons, 1966). As age increases, social participation decreases; older citizens also increase their religious activities and dependence upon

27

religion. This fact alone should reinforce a conservative position with regard to public order crimes, since there is a clear allusion of "immorality" in biblical reference to public order criminals--especially homosexuals. Besides these things, a social-psychological distance between the old and the young in American society seems to exist today, and the nature of the distance appears to be defined by the younger generation (Von Mering, 1968). As a research prognostication, <u>younger respondents should be more favorable toward decriminalization of public order crimes than older respondents.</u>

Religion, the fifth independent variable, is commonly assumed to reflect American core-values based upon the Protestant Ethic. This Ethic, embodied in the traditional teachings of institutionalized and primarily Protestant religions, articulates hard work and a meticulous adherence to religious and moral concepts (Weber, 1958). Religious correlations have been substantiated within a broad range of studies; religion and the world of work (Lenski, 1961); religious intolerance (Glock and Stark, 1969); and religious affiliation and family solidarity (Dankel, 1944). We anticipate therefore, that more orthodox religious affiliation will be directly related to receptivity for innovation and change in the criminal code.[34] <u>Orthodox Protestants will be expected to show more tolerance than Catholics and other religious groups toward public order crime and changes in criminal laws.</u>

Statement of Hypotheses

As indicated earlier in the chapter, the first objective of the present study is to test hypotheses regarding the two dimensions of the social reaction concept: (1) knowledge of public order criminals (belief component) and (2) decriminalization of these laws (behavior component). Based on the results of previous studies and the general labeling theoretical orientation, a positive correlation between beliefs about deviance (knowledge contingency) and decriminalization and punishment contingency, is expected. The specific hypotheses to be examined are summarized below:

28

Hypothesis 1. A substantial positive correlation exists between high knowledge in deviance perception and legal decriminalization of public order crimes.

Hypothesis 2. A substantial positive correlation exists between high knowledge in deviance perception and low applications of stigma (labeling) or punishment.

Hypothesis 3. "Deviance-perception crystallization" (DPC) will occur, i.e., respondents who are intolerant toward one deviant group will tend to be intolerant toward other deviant groups.

Hypothesis 4. High SES level will be directly related to legal decriminalization of public order crimes.

Hypothesis 5. High SES level will be inversely related to the application of punishment for public order crimes.

Hypothesis 6. Age will be inversely related to legal decriminalization of public order criminal laws.

Hypothesis 7. Age will be directly related to the application of punishment for public order crimes.

Hypothesis 8. Males will demonstrate more positive attitudes toward public order crime decriminalization and will be less punitive than females.

Hypothesis 9. Protestant religious affiliation will be directly related to legal decriminalization of public order crimes to a greater extent than will Catholic and other religious group affiliation.

Hypothesis 10. Protestant religious affiliation will be inversely related to the application of punitive sanction. Catholic and other religious group affiliation will not.

Hypothesis 11. Urban residence will be positively associated with legal decriminalization of public order crimes and low applications of punishment.

RESEARCH DESIGN AND METHODOLOGY

The Sample

The present study is an analysis of data on criminal law decriminalization collected from a random sample of Lewiston, Idaho residents during the first part of 1973. Lewiston is located in Nez Perce County at the confluence of the Snake and Clearwater Rivers and has a population of 26,068, which includes the recently incorporated suburban district of Lewiston Orchards. Lewiston is an important trading and industrial center serving a region known for its agriculture, forestry, and mining. Local manufactures are primarily involved in production of wood products such as paper, lumber and pulp. The homogeneity of the community is demonstrated by the absence of any sizable racial or ethnic minority. Together, minority groups comprise less than one-half of one percent of the total population.

Data Collection

The sample was drawn by a systematic random procedure based on a sample cluster of housing units per voting precinct.[35] The data device was a questionnaire personally distributed by an interviewer to each household. The purpose of the inquiry was explained and respondents were asked to complete the questionnaire and return it by mail. A total of 400 questionnaires were distributed and 258 were returned, indicating a return rate of 64.5 percent. Although this is a reasonably satisfactory level of return and is considered typical of such studies (Oppenheim, 1966), it does not negate the possibility of nonresponse bias. Nine questionnaires were discarded due to incomplete information, resulting in a final number of 249 (60.1 percent) usable forms. This number represents a one percent specific sample population.

Definition and Measurement of Variables

The basic question that the study asks is whether community consensus on criminal conceptions is associated with consensus to delete public order crimes from

criminal statutes. The measuring instrument was the structured questionnaire form.
The questionnaire item format was adapted and patterned after Rooney and Gibbon's
(1966) study on social tolerance toward victimless crimes.[36] Items form fixed-
alternative Likert-type questions in which respondents were asked to indicate the
degree to which they would approve of modifications in social policies toward public
order crimes. A few items concerned related matters of alcoholism, police policies
and kindred topics. Other questions were limited to those necessary only for clarification of answers. The purpose and design of the questionnaire was to evoke or
elicit an exact response on issues considered by some to be controversial, and to
establish as lucid a communication as was possible using the questionnaire method of
data collection.[37]

Dependent Variables

The two dependent variables used in the study are legal decriminalization
and the contingency of punishment, both integral conceptual elements of the social
reaction hypothesis in labeling theory. Legal decriminalization is defined as community consensus to remove public order crimes (abortion, prostitution, homosexuality,
and narcotic laws) from criminal codes. Essentially, this measure is indicative of a
behavioral response comparable to an individual casting a "vote" or ballot in a
public referendum or election. It should be understood, however, that this measure is
clearly a behavioral expectation rather than a behavioral outcome.

Legal Decriminalization

The dependent variable legal decriminalization was measured by 15 questions
forming four sub-scales or indexes. For each question, values of 1, 2, 3, or 4 were
assigned to the responses in Likert fashion. Those responses which most strongly
agreed with proposals to liberalize existing policies were given a score of 4, while
those which most markedly disagreed with these proposals were given a score of 1.
More complex scoring has been shown to possess no advantage (Oppenheim, 1966). The
"index" scale was computed by the method of combining several questions relating to

31

one specific public order crime. There is a sub-scale index for all subsequent criminal categories. The basic assumption of the scales are that an individual's position on the scale index should indicate either positive or negative attitudes toward decriminalizing legal statutes. Further, a master or summary index was computed inclusive of all four forms of deviance, assuming approximation between the larger summary measure as an expression of a "global" cross-dimensional index score, or statistical convergence. A sample of questions from each sub-category is given below (questions 3, 4, 14, 30 on Questionnaire, Appendix C).

Abortion

It is a medical fact that in about one-third of the cases where a pregnant woman contacts German measles within the first 12 weeks of her pregnancy, various abnormalities result to the child. These include cataracts, deafness, microcephaly, and heart lesions. A pregnant woman who has German measles should be allowed to have an abortion, if she wishes one.

Prostitution

Prostitution should be legalized and licensed so that prostitutes would be allowed to work at their trade in certain districts of the city.

Homosexuality

From time to time, recommendations have been made to the effect that the criminal laws against homosexual acts should be changed. If the laws were revised, acts of homosexual behavior between consenting adult partners would not be illegal. The laws should be so modified. Persons should be allowed to be homosexuals if they so desire.

Narcotics

Existing narcotics laws in Idaho have the effect of making the use of opium, heroin, cocaine, and other opium derivatives for other than medical reasons illegal. These laws should be continued, and if anything they should be strengthened.

The summary (Master) index scale is a substantially improved measure over the category mean scores used by Rooney and Gibbons (1966), Gilbert (1958), Gibbons (1969), and Rose and Prell (1955). Measurement is promoted by similarities in the overall pattern of relationship. The interitem correlation in the study was computed at .541, which yields a coefficient of reliability of .946 for the dependent variable law change. This measure denotes high internal consistency of index items (content validity) or uni-dimensionality in summated scales.[38]

Contingency of Punishment

In order to measure the punishment contingency construct in the social reaction concept, fictional cases of criminality involving public order criminal activity were employed and respondents were asked to select the penalties they considered appropriate for individuals described in these incidents. The operational measure was arbitrarily determined by a dichotomous classification: (1) punishment by incarceration; or (2) non-punitive treatment methods. Questions form an index of a person's position on a scale ranging from a purely punitive reaction or policy toward public order criminals to a purely treatment reaction or policy. In turn, reactions were compared to existing legal statutes on public order crimes to assess the severity of punishment.[39] An example of the contingency of punishment type question on narcotics is outlined below.

> Bill Bishop is a 25-year old male who lives in a cheap hotel in the downtown area of city X. The police get a "tip" that Bishop is a narcotics user. They manage to get into Bishop's hotel room where they surprise him in the act of flushing several capsules of heroin down the toilet. They also find a hypodermic needle below the window of his room. He is arrested and taken to court on charges of "possession of narcotics." His previous arrest record shows that he has been convicted of two instances of petty theft, but no previous drug charges. He is convicted of the narcotics charge in this instance.
>
> If you were in a position to decide the question, which of the sentences or dispositions below do you believe would be the most reasonable in this case? Check the appropriate sentence.

Score

__1__	Execution
__2__	Prison sentence of over 10 years but less than 15 years
Punishment __3__	Prison sentence of over 5 years but less than 10 years
__4__	Prison sentence of over 1 year but less than 5 years
__5__	Jail term of six months in length
__6__	Jail term of one month in length

	7	Probation and supervision by a probation officer
Treatment	8	Fine of around $100 without bail or probation
	9	No penalty
	10	Other: If treatment oriented recommendations

High scores on the scale are equated with a more lenient treatment orientation.

A similar procedure utilized in measuring legal decriminalization was adopted for the contingency of punishment measure. Internal relations among various sub-index public order crime criteria were examined to ascertain whether they were theoretically interrelated as expected and if statistical convergence occurred. Interitem correlations computed in the summated (Master) index averaged .352 resulting in a content validity of .62. This figure indicates low item internal consistency or homogeneity and falls substantially below the .95 one would expect to obtain unidemsionality in a summated scale. By itself this scale would be quite weak. When it is considered in concert with legal decriminalization as a co-measure in calibrating the social reaction hypothesis the weakness is somewhat reduced. It brings to the surface, however, a problem inherent in any attempt to operationalize a new conceptual system in terms of appropriate criteria or measures. Construct validity is the most important criterion for the development of empirical measures of knowledge and punishment contingencies in the social reaction concept in validation of labeling theory. Because of the centrality of construct validity in the attempt to achieve integration of labeling theoretical propositions in the study, the concept warrants further attention.

Construct Validity

Construct validity, according to Selltiz, et al. (1967), brings in other evidence to provide a basis for judging whether the measuring instrument adequately measures the concept it is intended to measure. Examination of construct validity involves validation not only of the measuring instrument but of the theory behind it.

> Construct validity cannot be adequately tested by any single procedure. Evidence from a number of sources is relevant . . . . The validity of the test depends on the relationships predicted in the theoretical network in which the construct is embodied.

The more different relationships tested and confirmed, the greater the support both for the measuring instrument and for the underlying theory (Selltiz, et al., 1967:163).

The ultimate goal of such validative procedures in the view of Cronbach and Meehl (1955), is to imbed the new construct or test in a nomological net or interlying system of laws which constitute a theory. The theoretical network includes various sub-variables such as social background correlates and how they are related to other attitudinal or perceptual variables and to some aspects of behavior.

Extending from the discussion of construct validity the importance of this concept becomes clear with respect to labeling theory. If the summated index scales and social reaction components are logically and consistently related to labeling theory, results can be interpreted and can lead to future hypotheses in the same theoretical context. The knowledge contingency independent variable and research social correlates form the propositional set or predictive network of relationships from which construct validity is inferred.

Independent Variables

Knowledge Contingency

The major independent variable in the study is the knowledge contingency in deviance perception. Scale items on this variable test respondent's conception of deviants against social scientific information about deviants discussed in the first part of the chapter.[40] Index scores, both sub-index and cross-dimensional, form the knowledge contingency. The operationalization of knowledge contingency is the degree to which a respondent possesses the "knowledge" concerning public order deviants measured by these items. A set of 12 index items comprise the summated or master index and may be called a global measure, or deviance perception crystallization (DPC). These are further correlated with the punishment dependent variable to clarify it as a conceptually relevant measure. An example of a question from each public order crime index follows below (Questions 25, 31, 2, and 19, Appendix C).

Abortion

Most abortions in the United States are performed upon young unmarried girls.

Prostitution

One thing to be said in favor of prostitution is that it keeps the number of sex crimes lower.

Homosexuality

Most homosexuals are easy to "spot" because of the way they dress, walk, talk, or due to their occupations.

Narcotics

It is next to impossible for a drug addict to keep a legitimate job, since while he is under the influence of drugs he is unable to pay attention, to be alert, and so on.

In knowledge contingency questions, as in measures on dependent variables, individuals place themselves on an attitude continuum for each statement--from "strongly agree" to "strongly disagree." A high score on the Likert scale indicates high knowledge.

Other Independent Variables

For purposes of the study community size and age variables are replications of the U.S. Bureau of Census classifications and categories. In addition, information on residence background was solicited to more accurately determine if respondents were from Idaho or were more rural than urban. Residence background questions indicate whether the respondent was "raised in Idaho and lived in Idaho the majority of his life," "raised in a rural or urban area," or lived in Idaho for "10 years or more," "5 to 9 years," or "less than 5 years," and so forth. Duncan's (1967) socio-economic grouping of occupations, originally proposed to measure socio-economic status (SES) characteristics of sample respondents, cannot be used due to large scale nonresponses to the occupation category. Instead, education and income variables are interrelated and correlated as an indice of this dimension.[41]

Statistical Techniques

The Multiple Regression Linear Model

The statistical measures of association appropriate for data in this analysis are the Pearson product moment correlation (r) and the multiple coefficient of determination R^2. The term multiple correlation indicates how much of the total variation in the dependent variables (in this case criminal law decriminalization and punishment contingency) can be explained by all of the independent variables acting together simultaneously (Blalock, 1972). The only necessary assumption is that data be of interval level of measurement, which is affirmed for the data in this study.[42]

The linear statistical model for interval level data may be stated as

$$Y_i = B_0 + B_1 X_{i1} + \ldots + B_k X_{ik} + E_i.$$

R^2 measures the coterminous power of the independent variables, written to the right of the equal sign, to explain or predict the value of the dependent variable, Y. This function is referred to as the proportion of explained variation. It is also a measure of the relative reduction in prediction error achieved by basic line prediction.

Several problems are confronted in using the linear model, however, when specific independent variables are less than interval, as in the present study. Since this is the case, these variables are treated as nominal in the linear model and the measure of association is called E^2. Carlson (1972:34) has summarized this approach well:

> When the independent variables are not measured on an interval level they are treated as nominal in the linear model. The only difference is that the X_1's are coded with either 0 or 1, rather than with interval level values. In this situation the value of B_0 is no longer an intercept in the conventional sense. It is the expected value of Y under specified conditions. These conditions are specified by the researcher in the way he sets up his model, but the expectation equals the expected value of Y when $X_i = X_j$, for all i and j . . . . In using the linear model for cases like this it is customary to call the measure of association E^2 rather than R^2. Clearly, the only distinction between the two coefficients is that E^2 does not specify a specific form the relation must take. Some writers refuse to use separate names in as much as the underlying logic is identical. . . .

This approach will be followed in the present study and all measures of association will be called R^2. Nominal variables affected by this procedure are the residence classification, sex differentiation, and religious affiliation. In setting up the model they were coded as:[43]

Residence:	Urban = 0
	Rural = 1
Sex:	Male = 0
	Female = 1
Religion:	Protestant = 0
	Other = 1

Procedures

The procedures followed in the study begin with computation of bivariate zero order correlations (r) to ascertain the direction and magnitude of relationships. Next the study will examine the influence of interaction[44] effects of independent variables in competition with each other to determine which have the strongest relationship with the dependent variable in terms of the amount of explained variation each contributes. This provides a cumulative measure of how much variation of the dependent variable can be accounted for by controlling for interrelations (overlap). In determining the effects of index variables and subsets of variables, partial coefficients of determination and standardized regression (beta) coefficients will be used to measure the PRE in Y which occurs due to x_j after the other variables have explained all they can. This yields a correlation between any two variables when the effects of other variables have been controlled.

The F-ratio is used as a test of significance for the R^2 measure to examine the fit of the entire multiple regression model. The F-ratio measures the ratio of the two estimates of the population variance: the ratio of the between-group sum of squares (explained variation) to the within-group sum of squares (unexplained variation). As a significance test of R^2 the F-ratio determines whether the magnitude of R^2 is statistically probable in order to conclude that the hypothesized variable relationships were not due to chance factors. As R^2 approaches 1, the F value becomes progressively larger.

CHAPTER 5

ANALYSIS OF THE DATA

This chapter is concerned with the assessment and evaluation of research findings on the social processes which occur in society's response to those who are different, deviant, or for other reasons are subject to social and legal intervention. We stated earlier that the labeling approach suggests that criminally defined behaviors are social definitions and not intrinsic qualities of a given act. If these assumptions are valid and the inferences made are subjected to critical examination, then such definitions should vary in the kind and amount of reactions they receive from the public and the society as a whole. Labeling theoretical explications may therefore be directly related to changes in the criminal law, to criminal conceptions, and, in general, to the broad processes of making and applying legal rules. Following this line of inquiry, we would expect to find community consensus on criminal definitions and conceptions to be associated with willingness of community members to modify controversial criminal laws.

Legal Decriminalization

The research reported on here sought to establish whether or not a population believed public order kinds of crime should be decriminalized or removed from legal statutes. It has long been generally assumed that the public believes criminal laws dealing with public order deviants are appropriate measures for controlling these kinds of criminal behaviors. Examination of dimensions of community response for legal deletion of victimless laws offers relatively little support for this notion. In fact, a majority of the population studied considered three of these crimes (abortion,[45] prostitution,[51] and homosexuality) as subject to removal from the criminal codes. In Table 5.1 community consensus for legal decriminalization of abortion laws is presented. The table shows that 79 percent of respondents favor abortion for women who contact German measles during pregnancy, 75 percent when women can show through expert psychiatric testimony that they are psychologically disturbed, and 92 percent favored abortion when women become pregnant as a result of rape or incest. Without question, the data support the conclusion that citizens overwhelmingly favor more liberal as opposed to punitive abortion policies and laws.

Changes in laws on homosexual behavior are also conceded a fairly wide base of support. Over 54 percent of sample members believed that these laws should be modified so that homosexual conduct between consenting adults in private would be legal. Social consensus to legalize private consensual sexual conduct does not necessarily infer that public order deviants such as homosexuals are no longer widely rejected by the population. The fact that few respondents (39 percent) favored public recognition of overt forms of homosexual organization or of the practice of widespread employment of homosexuals in government or industry demonstrates that such behavior continues to be strongly sanctioned by the mores.

On the other hand, liberalization of prostitution in the criminal law would be commensurate and consistent with data dictates from the research. The legalization of prostitution seems to have more support (55 percent) than opposition among members of the sample. Modification of the law on the use of narcotics does not receive similar indulgence from the public, however.

Indications are that a majority of the public believes this kind of activity ought to be proscribed and penalized. For example, 71 percent of the respondents strongly endorsed a punitive policy with respect to physicians who become drug addicts. Although citizens obviously distinguish between the user of the drug and the pusher, as evidenced by a strong rehabilitative and treatment orientation, they would nevertheless eliminate the double standard in the handling of narcotic pushers. All drug pushers, whether addicted or not, would be subjected to some form of punitive treatment.[46] In general, there was extremely high (91 percent) indication that criminal laws on narcotic abuse should be strengthened. There was only minimal support (18 percent) for legalizing marijuana. At the same time, more than limited

TABLE 5.1.

PERCENTAGE OF CONSENSUS FOR LEGAL DECRIMINALIZATION OF ABORTION,
PROSTITUTION, HOMOSEXUAL, AND NARCOTIC LAWS
(N = 249)

Item	Yes %	(N)	No %	(N)	No Res. %	(N)
ABORTION						
1. Women who contract German measles during pregnancy should be allowed to have an abortion.	79.1	(197)	18.1	(45)	2.8	(7)
2. Women who can show through expert psychiatric testimony that they are psychologically disturbed should be allowed to have an abortion.	75.5	(188)	21.7	(54)	2.8	(7)
3. The existing laws on abortion should remain unchanged.	26.5	(66)	71.4	(178)	2.1	(5)
4. Women who become pregnant as a result of rape or incest should be allowed to have an abortion.	91.5	(228)	6.2	(20)	2.3	(6)
5. Abortions should be illegal under all circumstances.	4.8	(12)	92.9	(231)	2.3	(6)

Summated (Master) Index score = 20   Mean = 14.6   Std. Dev. = 3.2

PROSTITUTION

Item	Yes %	(N)	No %	(N)	No Res. %	(N)
9. Prostitution should be legalized in the state of Idaho.	54.6	(136)	43.3	(108)	2.1	(5)

Summated (Master) Index score = 4   Mean = 2.4   Std. Dev. = .9

HOMOSEXUALITY

Item	Yes %	(N)	No %	(N)	No Res. %	(N)
6. Homosexuals should be allowed to organize in order to obtain the civil liberties they are denied.	38.5	(96)	56.6	(141)	4.9	(12)
7. The laws should be changed so that homosexual conduct between consenting adults would be legal.	54.6	(136)	41.7	(104)	3.7	(9)
8. A homosexual would not be a desirable employee in government or industry.	56.2	(140)	40.6	(101)	3.2	(8)

Summated (Master) Index score = 12   Mean = 6.7   Std. Dev. = 2.1

TABLE 5.1. - Continued

Item	Yes %	(N)	No %	(N)	No. Res. %	(N)

NARCOTICS

Item	Yes %	(N)	No %	(N)	No. Res. %	(N)
10. Physicians and pharmacists who become drug addicts should have their licenses revoked and be heavily punished.	71.4	(178)	21.7	(54)	6.9	(19)
11. Physicians should be allowed to treat drug addiction in the same way they treat other illnesses.	77.1	(192)	20.6	(51)	2.3	(6)
12. Both the addict-peddler and the non-addict-peddler should be subjected to the same form of punishment.	77.9	(194)	21.7	(54)	.4	(1)
13. The existing narcotics laws in Idaho should be strengthened.	91.1	(227)	6.6	(16)	2.3	(6)
14. More programs like Synanon are needed.	73.9	(184)	4.4	(11)	21.7	(54)
15. Marijuana should be legalized for adults.	18.1	(45)	79.6	(198)	2.3	(6)

Summated (Master) Index score = 24   Mean = 12.3   Std. Dev. = 2.8

concessions (77 percent) were in evidence for adoption of drug programs in which physicians would be allowed to treat drug addiction in the same way they treat other illnesses.

Although these findings do not tell us what criteria should be taken into account in determining what kinds of behavior should be treated as criminal, they do describe social reactions as being differentially distributed in a population, at the very least. Apparently legal norms do not prescribe the appropriate reactions for the total range of public order kinds of deviance previously defined as criminal. If this is so, crime is not an absolute concept as embodied in criminal laws, but is, essentially, a relative definition of behavior subject to the vagaries of time and circumstance. Definitions of crime are constantly and continually changing. It may be that we have some glimmerings that the public appears willing to tolerate more deviance today than it did previously.

In the remainder of the chapter some processes believed related to the generation and perpetuation of criminal conceptions will be examined. Bivariate cor-relations and multiple regression analysis were employed to test the relative influence and the degree of association of each of ten independent variables on the tendency to decriminalize public order legal statutes.

Bivariate Correlations

The bivariate correlation coefficients between the independent variables and legal decriminalization appear in Table 5.2. Data in the table assess the direction and strength of variable relationships in hypothesis one of the knowledge contingency; hypothesis four on socio-economic status; hypothesis six on age; hypothesis eight on sex differentiation; and hypotheses nine and eleven on religious affiliation and place of residence.

TABLE 5.2.

THE BIVARIATE RELATIONSHIP BETWEEN LEGAL DECRIMINALIZATION OF ABORTION, PROSTITUTION, HOMOSEXUAL, AND NARCOTICS LAWS AND TEN INDEPENDENT VARIABLES
(N = 249)

| Independent Variables | r | | | |
	Abortion	Prostitution	Homosexuality	Narcotics
Residence	-.038	-.109	-.027	-.049
Sex	-.053	-.235**	-.015	.020
Age	.185*	.048	.121	.146
Education	-.151	.038	-.199*	-.220**
Religious Affiliation	-.125	.031	.036	.220**
Income	.159*	.015	-.074	-.041
Knowledge	.158*	.014	.340**	.395**
Education and Income	.202*	.036	-.167*	.181*
Age and Knowledge	.246**	.074	.208*	.212**
Education and Knowledge	-.077	.060	-.091	.117

*Significant at the .05 level
**Significant at the .01 level

Knowledge Contingency

A positive correlation was stated to exist between the knowledge contingency

44

in deviance perception and legal decriminalization. Empirical regularities make this prediction plausible in that the correlation between knowledge and change in the criminal law is moderately large (r - .158, p <.05) and in the predicted direction. Correspondingly, knowledge was found to be significantly bound up with the tendency to decriminalize homosexual and narcotic laws (r - .340; .395), both statistically significant at the .01 level. When coefficients were squared (r^2) for these correlations, the knowledge variable accounted for 11 percent of the explained variance in homosexual laws and 14 percent in narcotic laws. These findings suggest that public beliefs about deviant behavior are tentatively indicative of social consensus to remove or delete legal statutes on victimless modes of crime and are consistent with theoretical postulates in the labeling model.

Socio-Economic Status and Legal Decriminalization

The zero order correlations between the combined variables of education and income, which indicate socio-economic status in the study, are significantly high (.05 level) for abortion, homosexuality and narcotic type crimes (r = .246, .203, and .212, respectively). The predicted relationship of high socio-economic status with toleration for modifications in criminal laws appears strongly supported. Education and income, taken separately, are also indicators of socio-economic status. Education is significantly related to innovations in narcotics laws (r - .220, p < .01) and homosexual laws, and income with alterations in abortion laws (r - .159, p <.05). Together these measures convincingly cluster as a solid base and point to the possible predictive efficacy of the socio-economic status variable with new legal forms.

Age and Legal Decriminalization

Although age was hypothesized to be directly related to legal decriminalization of public order crimes, the only statistically significant correlation coefficient for this variable was with abortion law change (r = .185, p <.05). The low or near zero correlations for the age variable in all crime categories suggests that the old and the young are equally likely to decriminalize prostitution and homosexual laws.

Younger persons have moderately higher positive associations with narcotic law changes (r = .146).

Sex and Legal Decriminalization

The association of the independent variable sex with legal modifications in criminal laws followed similar patterns across all forms of public order crimes. As predicted, males (negative correlations) were more strongly correlated with decriminalization of these crimes. Urban males also had the highest propensity to modify prostitution laws (r = -.109 and -.235). The sex variable was significant at the .01 level.

Religious Affiliation and Legal Decriminalization

Protestant religious affiliation was predicted to be directly related to legal decriminalization of public order crimes to a greater extent than Catholic and other religious group affiliation. Bivariate correlations, however, denote that this independent variable is only tenable for expectancies and variations in narcotic law crime categories (r - .220, p < .01). Moreover, the direction of the relationship is inverse rather than direct as expected; that is, individuals who are either Catholic or who are not affiliated with any traditional "institutional" religious organization are much more receptive than Protestants to legal reform involving narcotic laws.

Place of Residence and Legal Decriminalization

Hypothesis eleven stated that there would be a positive correlation between urban place of residence and legal change. The hypothesis also stated that rural residence would be inversely related to changes in criminal codes. While few of the correlation coefficients in Table 5.2 can be considered strong, the table does show that the expected direction of hypothesized correlations did occur. (It will be recalled that in setting up the linear model nominal variables were coded in such a way that negative correlations equaled positive relationships for the urban residence classification.) Urban residence was weakly but positively related to legal decriminalization on all four forms of deviant behavior studied (r - -.038, -.109, -.027, and

46

-.049).

Deviance Perception Crystallization

To test the third hypothesis on deviance perception, all four forms, or sub-indexes, of public order crime were examined to ascertain whether they were theoretically interrelated as expected and if statistical convergence took place. Statistical convergence in the cross-dimensional measure includes scores for each crime category and designates either a single predictor variable, or combination of predictor variables, most optimal and influential in explaining variance in the dependent variable. When the several subscales are combined, the measure of influence is representative of an individual's overall (global) profile on deviance perception. The advantages of this procedure, primarily, are that interaction effects eventuate in a final rank ordering of independent variables. Statistical convergence, if significant, increases confidence that construct validity is present.

Table 5.3 presents correlation coefficients for the summary master index. Quite clearly, the knowledge independent variable in deviance perception is manifest as the most salient predictor of public inclinations to decriminalize public order criminal laws ($r = .471$, $p < .01$). Statistically significant correlations at the .01 level were obtained for age ($r - .217$), and age and knowledge combined ($r = .292$), and for education and income and education at the .05 level of significance. These findings can be interpreted to mean that levels of social tolerance for legal reforms are related to public knowledge about and reaction to the four forms of criminal offense and to variations in the social background of the respondents. Younger, more educated persons exhibit greater approval of changes in social policies toward public order crimes than do other members of the sample population.

Although the data thus far suggest that the basic hypotheses are sound when bivariate correlations are computed between only one independent with the dependent variable, no conclusions can be drawn until controls are established for independent effects of statistical interaction. Consequently, we turn to Tables 5.4 through 5.8

47

TABLE 5.3.

THE BIVARIATE RELATIONSHIP BETWEEN A SUMMATED (MASTER) INDEX ON LEGAL
DECRIMINALIZATION OF PUBLIC ORDER CRIMES AND TEN INDEPENDENT VARIABLES
(N = 249)

Independent Variables	r
Residence	-.051
Sex	-.046
Age	.217**
Education	-.192*
Religious Affiliation	.017
Income	-.119
Knowledge	.471**
Education and Income	-.204*
Age and Knowledge	.292**
Education and Knowledge	.087

*Significant at the .05 level
**Significant at the .01 level

where the correlations between the independent variables and legal decriminalization
are presented in the multiple regression model.

In order to minimize the possibility of making spurious inferences, the coefficient of regression (beta) was used as a means of statistically controlling for
other, possibly confounding, variables.[47] A t-test was computed as a significance
test for the beta measure. The assumptions and rational behind use of the t-test are
described by Hamblin (1968:15):

> The test for significance of zero order correlations leads to
> Type 1 errors, particularly in the case when the effects of the
> independent variable are weak . . . . Theoretically, the t-test
> for regression coefficients is the best criterion of significance
> . . . . A t-value equal to or greater than 2.0 indicates signifi-
> cance at the .05 level . . . . With a reasonable measurement error,
> say 2 percent, Type 1 errors almost never occur.[48]

The results of multiple correlation and regression coefficient computations are discussed separately for each dependent variable.

Abortion Laws

Examining Table 5.4 on abortion laws we find that multiple regression analysis provides a close fit to the data. Although religious affiliation was a weak zero order correlation, it becomes a significant factor (p $<$ .01) in explaining variation in the dependent variable when the influence of other variables is controlled. The fact that religious affiliation (Protestant) is highly correlated with legal decriminalization of abortion laws comes as no great surprise in view of the theological nature of the controversy surrounding the sanctity of the fetus as a human life to be protected by criminal law. What is surprising is the obviously more liberal attitude of males toward abortion reform than females. Most of the variation in the dependent variable is a direct effect of the influence of young (25-34), urban college educated, Protestant males. The coefficient of determination (R^2 = .13) is highly significant (p $<$ .001), indicating that these variables explain 13 percent of the variance in abortion laws. The direction of the hypothesized relationships are rectilinear in support of the linear model.

TABLE 5.4.

MULTIPLE REGRESSION ANALYSIS AND STATISTICS OF FIT FOR LEGAL
DECRIMINALIZATION OF ABORTION LAWS AND TEN INDEPENDENT VARIABLES
(N = 249)

Source	Degrees of Freedom	Sum of Squares	Mean Squares	R	R^2	F	p
Regression of Independent Variables	10	360.74	36.07	.37	.13	3.78	.001
Error	238	2269.81	9.53				
Total	248	2630.56					

Independent Variables	Beta	t	Partial	Proportion Var. Cum.
Residence	-1.26581	-1.42450	-0.09195	0.00147
Sex	-0.70284	-1.73857	-0.11199	0.00309
Age	-0.53073	-0.81621	-0.05283	0.03832
Education	0.75866	0.94261	0.06099	0.01508
Religious Affiliation	-1.28233	-2.86618**	-0.18266	0.02665
Income	-0.13022	-0.60308	-0.03906	0.02124
Knowledge	0.11601	0.29893	0.01937	0.01481
Education and Income	-0.03046	-0.39374	-0.02551	0.00051
Age and Knowledge	0.13373	1.54002	0.09933	0.01006
Education and Knowledge	-0.12914	-1.27640	-0.08245	0.00591

**Significant at the .01 level

Prostitution Laws

Public dispositions toward legal innovations in prostitution laws can be explained, in part, on the basis of the influence of a predictor variable whose relation with legal decriminalization we have studied. Table 5.5 reveals that the zero order correlation of sex (male) remained significantly correlated with the dependent variable when standardized beta weights were used. In addition to sex, however, the variable urban residence also becomes predominent. Thus, we find that the linear relationship suggests additivity of effect between legal decriminalization of prostitution and urban males. T-tests were significant at the .01 level for males and .05 level for urban residence. This indicates that significant zero order correlations may also prove to be associated in an important fashion with the dependent variable after the partial correlations have been computed. The value of R^2 (= .08) is interpreted to mean that by knowledge of the sex and residence of an individual we could reduce our error in predicting the probability of decriminalization of prostitution criminal laws by about 8 percent. Actually, this is quite low.

TABLE 5.5.

MULTIPLE REGRESSION ANALYSIS AND STATISTICS OF FIT FOR LEGAL
DECRIMINALIZATION OF PROSTITUTION LAWS AND TEN INDEPENDENT VARIABLES
(N = 249)

Source	Degrees of Freedom	Sum of Squares	Mean Squares	R	R^2	F	p
Regression of Independent Variables	10	20.94	2.09	.29	.08	2.30	.05
Error	238	216.33	0.90				
Total	248	237.28					

Independent Variables	Beta	t	Partial	Proportion Var. Cum.
Residence	-1.26581	-1.42450	-0.09195	0.00147
Sex	-0.70284	-1.73857	-0.11199	0.00309
Age	-0.53073	-0.81621	-0.05283	0.03832
Education	0.75866	0.94261	0.06099	0.01508
Religious Affiliation	-1.28233	-2.86618**	-0.18266	0.02665
Income	-0.13022	-0.60308	-0.03906	0.02124
Knowledge	0.11601	0.29893	0.01937	0.01481
Education and Income	-0.03046	-0.39374	-0.02551	0.00051
Age and Knowledge	0.13373	1.54002	0.09933	0.01006
Education and Knowledge	-0.12914	-1.27640	-0.08245	0.00591

*Significant at the .05 level
**Significant at the .01 level

Homosexual Laws

Table 5.6 shows the beta relationships between independent variables and homosexual laws. It seems clear that bivariate correlations once independently associated with these laws recede when interaction effects are controlled. The general pattern that emerges makes explicit the contribution of the knowledge contingency in the perception of deviance and estimations of social response (beta - .26, $p < .01$). Further, age and education variables connote additivity of effect. As a result, the null hypothesis of no linear relation can be rejected at the .001 level of probability (R^2 = .15). Thus, by knowledge of an individual's beliefs concerning

TABLE 5.6.

MULTIPLE REGRESSION ANALYSIS AND STATISTICS OF FIT FOR LEGAL
DECRIMINALIZATION OF HOMOSEXUAL LAWS AND TEN INDEPENDENT VARIABLES
(N = 249)

Source	Degrees of Freedom	Sum of Squares	Mean Squares	R	R^2	F	p
Regression of Independent Variables	10	173.96	17.39	.39	.15	4.33	.001
Error	238	956.06	4.01				
Total	248	1130.03					

Independent Variables	Beta	t	Partial	Proportion Var. Cum.
Residence	-0.35577	-0.61826	-0.04004	0.00075
Sex	-0.02629	-0.09995	-0.00648	0.00028
Age	-0.21523	-0.72683	-0.04706	0.01580
Education	-0.13499	-0.32974	-0.02137	0.03312
Religious Affiliation	0.08354	0.28816	0.01868	0.00031
Income	0.02235	0.15944	0.01033	0.00164
Knowledge	0.26692	4.33531**	0.27054	0.09240
Education and Income	-0.02106	-0.41914	-0.02716	0.00051
Age and Knowledge	0.04089	1.06733	0.06902	0.00905
Education and Knowledge	-0.00711	-0.14609	-0.00947	0.00008

**Significant at the .01 level

public order homosexual deviants, concurrent with the age and the amount of education each experienced, the error in predicting public removal of restrictions on homosexual laws could be reduced by 15 percent.

Narcotic Laws

Narcotic laws are consistent with the patterns observed in homosexual laws, but more profoundly delineate the ascendance of the knowledge factor in public propensities to delete criminal laws on narcotic abuse. Among the ten variables considered in the regression model, knowledge explained most of the variation in the dependent variable (beta = .429). The null hypothesis is rejected beyond the .001 level of statistical significance. Following knowledge, the next most important

TABLE 5.7.

MULTIPLE REGRESSION ANALYSIS AND STATISTICS OF FIT FOR LEGAL DECRIMINALIZATION OF NARCOTICS LAWS AND TEN INDEPENDENT VARIABLES
(N = 249)

Source	Degrees of Freedom	Sum of Squares	Mean Squares	R	R^2	F	p
Regression of Independent Variables	10	493.43	49.34	.48	.23	7.39	.001
Error	238	1588.83	6.67				
Total	248	2082.26					

Independent Variables	Beta	t	Partial	Proportion Var. Cum.
Residence	-0.12128	-0.16313	-0.01057	0.00246
Sex	0.04307	0.12754	0.00827	0.00032
Age	-0.11562	-0.30174	-0.01956	0.02072
Education	-0.41032	-0.77928	-0.05045	0.03987
Religious Affiliation	1.23069	3.28618**	0.20834	0.04180
Income	0.17328	0.95949	0.06207	0.00002
Knowledge	0.42951	5.48054***	0.33476	0.12777
Education and Income	-0.05712	-0.88211	-0.05709	0.00232
Age and Knowledge	0.01235	0.24638	0.01597	0.00153
Education and Knowledge	0.01374	0.21907	0.01420	0.00015

**Significant at the .01 level
***Significant at the .001 level

variable was other religious affiliation, which was significantly correlated with legal decriminalization at the .01 level. The data suggest the tenable conclusion that certain types of religious values are expressed by persons who are outside the pale of denominational sectarian church membership. In agreement with Clausen (1971), it is not inconceivable that this turnabout is attributable to a privatizing of religious values. Variable relationships are in the predicted direction and goodness of fit for data are explicit in the linear model (R^2 = .23). The null hypothesis of no linear relation can be rejected at the .001 probability level.

Summated (Master) Index on Legal Decriminalization

The summated index, or global measure of deviance perception, provides a comprehensive summary of the relative influence and importance of specified independent variables in explaining the overall tendency to decriminalize public order laws. Comparing Table 5.8 and the summated index measure, the highest correlation, as may be seen, is between the knowledge variable (beta = .770, $p < .001$) and legal decriminalization. The next two most important variables are age and education ($R^2 = .29$, $p < .001$) which, together with knowledge, explain 29 percent of the variance in legal social change. When knowledge is considered separately, it is a relatively strong predictor of the probability of decriminalizing all four forms of public order deviant behavior studied. Extrapolating from these findings one might predict that the greater the extent of knowledge about public order criminals within a population the greater would be the proportion of that population willing to support legal changes in criminal laws. On the basis of the data described above some measure of support is given to this assertion.

By use of the linear model in evaluation of social reaction hypotheses as labeling theoretical postulates, statistical convergence with the theoretical model becomes increasingly evident. Similar to Rooney and Gibbon's (1966) findings on social background in relation to social tolerance for crimes without victims, certain consistent patterns in acceptance of law change are manifested in some of the group membership characteristics measured by the independent variables.[49] These also indicate construct validity. Essentially, younger persons, males, with some college education, and who do not hold stereotypic images of deviants are more likely to decriminalize public order crimes.

Overall, these findings appear tenable and consistent with the theoretical propositions in the study. The null hypothesis of no population multiple correlation can be rejected with little apprehension of Type 1 error. On the basis of the foregoing discussion, we can conclude that the knowledge contingency in deviance perception

TABLE 5.8.

MULTIPLE REGRESSION ANALYSIS AND STATISTICS OF FIT
FOR A SUMMATED (MASTER) INDEX ON LEGAL DECRIMINALIZATION
OF PUBLIC ORDER CRIMES AND TEN INDEPENDENT VARIABLES
(N = 249)

Source	Degrees of Freedom	Sum of Squares	Mean Squares	R	R^2	F	p
Regression of Independent Variables	10	3581.64	358.16	.54	.29	9.85	.001
Error	238	8651.35	36.35				
Total	248	12233.0					

Independent Variables	Beta	t	Partial	Proportion Var. Cum.
Residence	-1.79570	-1.03617	-0.06701	0.00268
Sex	-0.73583	-0.93052	-0.06021	0.00248
Age	0.79665	0.85640	0.05543	0.05176
Education	1.61443	1.30079	0.08402	0.02530
Religious Affiliation	-0.91711	-1.04814	-0.06778	0.00051
Income	-0.07529	-0.17866	-0.01158	0.00739
Knowledge	0.77092	7.33400***	0.42935	0.17524
Education and Income	-0.06569	-0.43490	-0.02818	0.00083
Age and Knowledge	-0.03242	-0.26305	-0.01705	0.01486
Education and Knowledge	-0.29421	-1.98738	-0.12777	0.01174

***Significant at the .001 level

is the one best combination of several predictors for estimating future leanings in the direction of legal changes in victimless crimes.

Punishment Contingency

In Chapter 3 we postulated a theoretical bridge linking legal decriminalization with the punishment contingency construct, identifying social reaction as a useful theoretical concept in the sociological study of deviance. Punishment it will be recalled, is a behavioral expectation as well as an important part of social reaction. It is also a measure of the consistency or inconsistency, proportion or disproportion between stigma or punishment and the deviant attribute or action toward which they are

55

directed (Lemert, 1967). We also stated earlier that if a respondent defined legal behavior as deviant by agreeing with legally designated status (criminalization), but was not consistent in conferment of punitive treatment to the deviant as a result of that definition, the individual would not be sociologically deviant. Put differently, people who feel that present criminal laws controlling public order deviants should remain unchanged should punish deviants more severely than people who favor repeal of these criminal laws. To further test this general hypothesis, crimes which ranked lowest on the standard Likert scale mean scores were selected for further review.[50]

Public Order Crimes

Table 5.9 shows the percent of community consensus on punishment of narcotic crimes. A general perusal of the data discloses that a significant proportion (61 percent) of respondents recommended some type of punishment by incarceration over more lenient treatment considerations. A number of citizens (19 percent) advocated the extreme punishment measure allowed by law--a prison sentence of over 10 years but less than 15 years. Only a third of those sampled believed that some kind of treatment should follow heroin use. But the form of the treatment would be supervision by a probation officer rather than as a clinic outpatient.[51]

TABLE 5.9.

PERCENTAGE OF CONSENSUS FOR PUNISHMENT OF NARCOTIC CRIMES
(N = 249)

Punishment Contingency	%	N
Execution	2.8	7
Prison sentence of over 10 years but less than 15 years	19.3	48
Prison sentence of over 5 years but less than 10 years	5.2	13
Prison sentence of over 1 year but less than 5 years	20.5	51
Jail term of six months in length	11.2	28
Subtotal	61.4	153

TABLE 5.9. - Continued

Punishment Contingency		%	N
Treatment			
Probation and supervision by a probation officer		32.5	81
Fine of around $100 without jail or probation		0.8	2
No penalty		0	0
Other--treatment oriented recommendations		0.8	2
	Subtotal	34.2	85
No response		4.4	11
	Total	100.0	249

Community consensus on the punishment of marijuana crimes were far less punitive, however. Nearly fifty percent of the population studied (Table 5.10) agreed that marijuana cases should be handled by probation and supervision. Severe penalties were supported by only 10 percent of the community. Conversely, the general public took a more critical stance toward sexual deviation (see Table 5.11). Seventeen percent (N = 42) of sample members believed that homosexuals should be sentenced to prison for up to 15 years; a small minority (4 percent) opted for execution. These more extreme measures were balanced, in the main, by an overall treatment orientation. For example, 36 percent (N = 90) of respondents recommended that persons involved in homosexual conduct be given psychiatric care, suggesting community agreement on a "sick" view of this form of deviance. This is less severe than the minimum of probation specified by law. On the basis of the data described above, it is apparent that punishment patterns are differential in nature. In general, data indicate the existence of a strong to lenient continuum in the application of punitive sanction by the public. Narcotic and homosexual behavior are at the negative extreme and marijuana use at the other.

TABLE 5.10.

PERCENTAGE OF CONSENSUS FOR PUNISHMENT OF MARIJUANA CRIMES

Punishment Contingency	%	N
Execution	3.6	9
Prison sentence of over 10 years but less than 15 years	3.2	8
Prison sentence of over 5 years but less than 10 years	0.4	1
Prison sentence of over 1 year but less than 5 years	4.8	12
Jail term of six months in length	10.4	26
Subtotal	29.8	9
Treatment		
Probation and supervision by a probation officer	45.4	113
Fine of around $100 without jail or probation	10.4	26
No penalty	0	0
Other--treatment oriented recommendations	10.8	27
Subtotal	66.6	166
No response	3.6	9
Total	100.0	249

TABLE 5.11.

PERCENTAGE OF CONSENSUS FOR PUNISHMENT OF HOMOSEXUAL CRIMES

Punishment Contingency	%	N
Execution	4.4	11
Prison sentence of over 10 years but less than 15 years	16.9	42
Prison sentence of over 5 years but less than 10 years	0.8	2
Prison sentence of over 1 year but less than 5 years	6.4	16
Jail term of six months in length	4.8	12
Subtotal	34.1	85
Treatment		
Probation and supervision by a probation officer	17.7	44
Fine of around $100 without jail or probation	5.6	14
No penalty	0	0
Other--treatment oriented recommendations	36.1	90
Subtotal	59.4	148
No response	6.4	16
Total	100.0	249

Bivariate Correlations

A review of zero order correlations between independent variables and the punishment contingency indicate statistically significant relationships for only the marijuana category. Hypothesis two stated that there would be a substantial positive relationship between high knowledge in deviance perception and low applications of stigma or punishment. Examination of Table 5.12 points to a high degree of association between knowledge (r = .234, p < .001), the combined variables of age and knowledge (r = .290, p < .01), and education (r = -.169, p < .05) and low applications of stigma and punishment of marijuana smokers. Unexpectedly, low zero order correlations[52] obtain for the narcotics and homosexual punishment classification. Presumably, the regression line was suspected of being curvilinear. Results of a scattergram, however, affirmed a rectilinear relationship. Thus, although not significant, the correlations between the punishment contingency and sex for narcotic crimes and knowledge for homosexual crimes are in the predicted direction. In addition, the comprehensive summated index bivariate correlation (Table 5.13) diagnosed knowledge (r = .308) as the single significant (p < .01) global measure between the punishment contingency.

TABLE 5.12.

THE BIVARIATE RELATIONSHIP BETWEEN THE PUNISHMENT CONTINGENCY FOR NARCOTIC, MARIJUANA, AND HOMOSEXUAL CRIMES AND TEN INDEPENDENT VARIABLES
(N = 249)

Independent Variables	r		
	Narcotics	Marijuana	Homosexuality
Residence	.067	-.094	.046
Sex	-.127	.005	-.031
Age	-.073	.202	.005
Education	.036	-.160*	.006
Religious Affiliation	.089	.149	.037
Income	-.083	.029	-.034
Knowledge	.027	.234**	.138
Education and Income	.026	-.134	-.010
Age and Knowledge	-.013	.290**	.059
Education and Knowledge	.046	-.038	.038

*Significant at the .05 level
**Significant at the .01 level

59

TABLE 5.13.

THE BIVARIATE RELATIONSHIP BETWEEN A SUMMATED (MASTER) INDEX ON PUNISHMENT
CONTINGENCY OF PUBLIC ORDER CRIMES AND TEN INDEPENDENT VARIABLES
(N = 249)

Independent Variable	r
Residence	.044
Sex	.090
Age	.005
Education	-.018
Religious Affiliation	.013
Income	-.042
Knowledge	.308**
Education and Income	.013
Age and Knowledge	.074
Education and Knowledge	.026

**Significant at the .01 level

Narcotic Punishment Contingency

What is the relation between punishment contingency and each independent variable when the influences of the intercorrelations among these variables is eliminated? From Table 5.14 on narcotic punishment, it may be seen that the relationship between sex and the dependent variable is reduced. The variable of income (low) maintains the strongest relationship with narcotic punishment contingency when the effect of the other independent variables are partialled out (beta = .314). The t-test was significant at the .05 level. Beta regression coefficients and partial correlations, although not statistically significant, indicate that age (young), males, and "other" religious affiliation together explain the variance. The cumulative multiple R^2 is also statistically insignificant, however. These results may be attributable to attentuation due to restricted variance.

Marijuana Punishment Contingency

Bivariate correlations previously isolated three statistically significant relationships between the independent variables and the marijuana punishment

TABLE 5.14.

MULTIPLE REGRESSION ANALYSIS AND STATISTICS OF FIT FOR PUNISHMENT CONTINGENCY OF NARCOTICS CRIMES AND TEN INDEPENDENT VARIABLES
(N = 249)

Source	Degrees of Freedom	Sum of Squares	Mean Squares	R	R^2	F	p
Regression of Independent Variables	10	80.48	8.04	.25	.06	1.62	N.S.
Error	238	1181.68	4.96				
Total	248	1262.17					

Independent Variables	Beta	t	Partial	Proportion Var. Cum.
Residence	0.45958	0.71680	0.04641	0.00459
Sex	-0.46524	-1.59745	-0.10300	0.01524
Age	-0.60570	-1.83295	-0.11798	0.00284
Education	0.12168	0.26796	0.01737	0.00072
Religious Affiliation	0.50272	1.55654	0.10039	0.00854
Income	-0.31463	-2.02017*	-0.12984	0.00566
Knowledge	0.01221	0.18063	0.01171	0.00225
Education and Income	0.09889	1.77102	0.11405	0.01314
Age and Knowledge	0.06953	1.60793	0.10366	0.00661
Education and Knowledge	-0.05581	-1.03218	-0.06676	0.00419

*Significant at the .05 level

contingency--knowledge, age and knowledge jointly, and education. Of these variables, only knowledge (beta = .119, p $<$.02) remained strong and significant when other characteristics were controlled. Surprisingly, "other" religious affiliation had the next highest significant correlation (beta = .454, p $<$ .05). Accordingly, these findings may be interpreted to mean that high knowledge in deviance perception is associated with privatized religious values culminating in more tolerance for marijuana deviation. As with legal decriminalization, there is a tendency for those who perceive the deviant in terms other than stereotypes to be more tolerant. Conceivably, educational level is irrelevant in the case of the marijuana punishment.

TABLE 5.15.

MULTIPLE REGRESSION ANALYSIS AND STATISTICS OF FIT FOR PUNISHMENT
CONTINGENCY OF MARIJUANA CRIMES AND TEN INDEPENDENT VARIABLES
(N = 249)

Source	Degrees of Freedom	Sum of Squares	Mean Squares	R	R^2	F	p
Regression of Independent Variables	10	90.84	9.08	.40	.16	4.70	.001
Error	238	459.35	1.93				
Total	248	550.20					

Independent Variables	Beta	t	Partial	Proportion Var. Cum.
Residence	0.03172	0.07951	0.00515	0.00009
Sex	-0.00440	-0.02418	-0.00157	0.00002
Age	-0.20075	-0.98151	-0.06349	0.04181
Education	-0.10935	-0.38620	-0.02502	0.01764
Religious Affiliation	0.45456	2.26293*	0.14513	0.01513
Income	0.08473	0.87265	0.05648	0.00051
Knowledge	0.11901	3.11520**	0.19793	0.04561
Education and Income	-0.02620	-0.75232	-0.04871	0.00142
Age and Knowledge	0.04833	1.83247	0.11795	0.04273
Education and Knowledge	0.00698	0.20675	0.01340	0.00015

*Significant at the .05 level
**Significant at the .02 level

Homosexual Punishment Contingency

Comparable to the narcotic punishment contingency, the multiple R between homosexual crimes and independent variables does not closely fit the data and therefore statistical significance is not eminent (R^2 = .03). Even though the two dimensions of punishment with knowledge are correlated (beta = .190), they have low predictive power in the linear model. The data are contained in Table 5.16.

To summarize the conclusions of the section to this point, only in the case of the marijuana punishment contingency do we have criteria that should be taken into account in determining what kinds of behavior should be punished or treated

TABLE 5.16.

MULTIPLE REGRESSION ANALYSIS AND STATISTICS OF FIT FOR PUNISHMENT
CONTINGENCY OF HOMOSEXUAL CRIMES AND TEN INDEPENDENT VARIABLES
(N = 249)

Source	Degrees of Freedom	Sum of Squares	Mean Squares	R	R^2	F	p
Regression of Independent Variables	10	96.34	9.63	.17	.03	.75	N.S.
Error	238	3044.71	12.79				
Total	248	3141.06					

Independent Variables	Beta	t	Partial	Proportion Var. Cum.
Residence	0.48467	0.47197	0.03058	0.00216
Sex	-0.18645	-0.39713	-0.02573	0.00083
Age	-0.57395	-1.08609	-0.07023	0.00013
Education	0.46773	0.64021	0.04146	0.00003
Religious Affiliation	-0.31411	-0.60714	-0.03932	0.00156
Income	-0.08964	-0.35839	-0.02322	0.00070
Knowledge	0.19010	1.73020	0.11145	0.01883
Education and Income	0.02546	0.28397	0.01840	0.00038
Age and Knowledge	0.08032	1.17478	0.07593	0.00374
Education and Knowledge	-0.06528	-0.75200	-0.04869	0.00230

differentially. Furthermore, while the data presented above largely support the general hypotheses and theory set forth, the extent to which the probability of punishment is dependent on construct validity has not been demonstrated. These conclusions suggest restraint in interpreting the punishment contingency as applicable or predictive of behavioral expectancies toward narcotic or homosexual crimes.

Summated Master Index

An overview of the summated or global index is presented in Table 5.17. Two tentative conclusions can be drawn from a careful analysis of the table. First, a definite and significant association exists (beta = .429, $p < .001$) between high deviance perception (knowledge) crystallization and the probability of nonpunitive treatment. Second, regression coefficients, though not statistically significant by t-test

TABLE 5.17.

MULTIPLE REGRESSION ANALYSIS AND STATISTICS OF FIT FOR A SUMMATED (MASTER) INDEX ON PUNISHMENT CONTINGENCY OF PUBLIC ORDER CRIMES AND TEN INDEPENDENT VARIABLES
(N = 249)

Source	Degrees of Freedom	Sum of Squares	Mean Squares	R	R^2	F	p
Regression of Independent Variables	10	1087.81	108.78	.35	.12	3.37	.001
Error	238	7678.11	32.26				
Total	248	8765.93					

Independent Variables	Beta	t	Partial	Proportion Var. Cum.
Residence	0.95584	0.58596	0.03795	0.00199
Sex	-0.93289	-1.25654	-0.08118	0.00779
Age	-1.24137	-1.47254	-0.09502	0.00009
Education	0.72553	0.62674	0.04059	0.00035
Religious Affiliation	0.06465	0.07866	0.00510	0.00006
Income	-0.40694	-1.02507	-0.06631	0.00086
Knowledge	0.42947	4.63252***	0.28760	0.10271
Education and Income	0.15420	1.08370	0.07007	0.00435
Age and Knowledge	0.12369	1.11357	0.07199	0.00016
Education and Knowledge	-0.17182	-1.24661	-0.08054	0.00572

***Significant at the .001 level

standards, point to the contributing factors of sex (male), age (young), income, education and income, and age and knowledge in the amount of variance explained. The general tendency of the model is in the predicted direction and approximates good fit for the data (R^2 = .12, p < .001). These findings suggest that a recognition of social reaction as punishment contingency is generally related to the degree of consensus on social definitions of deviance. As Schur (1971:24) indicates, "a normative breach that could be but is not condemned or punished under existing formal laws is clearly less deviant than it would be if negative sanctions were actually applied." (Emphasis added.) The findings also hint, but do not strongly demonstrate, a more basic relationship between social structure and legal change. Significantly, it should be noted that both legal decriminalization and punishment contingency as dependent variables denote knowledge in deviance perception as the major predictor variable in accounting for the percentage of explained variance.

In recapitulation, Table 5.18 summarizes the proportion of variance explained by both summated indexes. It may be observed that the magnitude of the multiple correlation for legal decriminalization (R^2 = .29) indicates the model explains 29 percent of the variance in the dependent variable. Similarly, the model explains 12 percent of the variance in the punishment contingency. It seems reasonable then, to conclude at least tentative acceptance of the statistical model. If the prime gauge of the strength of a theory in science is goodness of fit to the data, or explained variance, then labeling theoretical postulations can be tentatively identified as certifiable in the study.[53]

TABLE 5.18.

RECAPITULATION: MULTIPLE REGRESSION ANALYSIS AND STATISTICS OF
FIT FOR SUMMATED (MASTER) INDEXES ON LEGAL DECRIMINALIZATION
AND PUNISHMENT CONTINGENCY AND TEN INDEPENDENT VARIABLES
(N = 249)

Dependent Variables	R	R^2	F-ratio	p
Legal Decriminalization	.54	.29	9.85	.001
Punishment Contingency	.35	.12	3.37	.05

In summary of the foregoing examination of study results, the following major empirical regularities concerning labeling propositions can be deduced. In general:

1. Socially defined criminal conceptions provide the groundwork for solidification of public consensus toward public order criminal law decriminalization and punitive sanctions. It is the interpretation others make of legally defined deviant behavior that is important rather than the behavior itself. Legal decriminalization of public order criminal behavior is therefore a function of public reaction to these acts rather than a function of the inherent qualities of

65

the act.

2. The nature and distribution of knowledge, or information, about a particular public order crime is a basic factor to be considered in explanations of definitions of deviance, and of societal reaction to deviance. Certain types of information (misconceptions) lead to more acts being defined as deviant.

3. Variations in social reaction to crime are a function of knowledge, or information, about public order criminals, a person's position in the social structure, age, and education. Knowledge, or information, concerning public order criminals is differentially distributed among higher socio-economic[54] status groups, college educated, younger persons. These persons will decriminalize public order type crimes to a greater extent than other members of the population. They are also likely to be less punitive toward public order lawbreakers.

Explanations and elaboration of these findings will be discussed in more detail in the following chapter.

CHAPTER 6

DISCUSSION OF RESULTS AND CONCLUSIONS

The nature of the relationship between public knowledge of deviance and social tolerance for legal decriminalization of public order crimes has been investigated in this study. The degree of punitive sanctions directed at offenders was also explored as a corollary hypothesis. Evidence was provided indicating that potential answers to the question of legal decriminalization reside in the nature of social knowledge and social response to deviance. It appears from the results that one major determinant of the predisposition to decriminalize legal statutes is knowledge, or information, about deviants. Conversely, the public does seem to hold stereotypical images of deviants and these images, or beliefs, are further removed from predispositions to action.

The likelihood that decriminalization will occur was basically related to social class variables, or social background characteristics of the persons who act as the definers of deviance. Public order crimes were likely to be regarded more tolerantly[55] by higher status members, with greater amounts of training and education, and by younger rather than older persons. There was also a positive social response by urban when compared to rural respondents and by men more than women. The likelihood of decriminalization occurring increases as community size and heterogeneity of the population increases. These findings are not inconsistent with past studies on labeling applications (e.g., Simmons, 1965; 1969; Rooney and Gibbons, 1966). Social definitions in societal reaction are thus seen to perpetuate labels that operate to increase probabilities of legal stigmatization. Components of the social reaction hypothesis therefore warrant attention in the development of integrated theorizing about deviance.

Research on understanding and explaining the societal reaction to lawbreaking rather than on lawbreaking itself reveals that criminal behavior, at least of the public order type, is a social construct. The reaction of a community to an act that results in a person's being labeled a deviant is consequently an important process in comprehending the nature of public order deviant behavior.

Labeling hypotheses were found to be congruent with explanations of deviant behavior as a social process; that is, deviant outcomes were attributable to the role of society and social values in defining the nature of criminal behavior. In this light, social reaction processes are concluded to affect the nature, distribution, and social meanings of crime. Thus, in the ongoing debate and controversy between labeling critics and polemics (discussed in Chapter Two), the findings of this research support the views of Schur (1969; 1971) over those of Gibbs (1966). Many of Gibbs' claims of "ambiguity" in the labeling approach are reduced by the degree to which empirical facts regarding social support for legal rules have become clarified here.

It seems equally clear that the study of public information and conceptions about "criminalized" deviant behavior has taken us one step beyond mere expression of agreement or disagreement with specific legal provisions (Schur, 1968). Research on the degree of public consensus on knowledge and definitions of deviance has indirectly enhanced our understanding of changes in the hierarchy of values in a society as reflected in the legal system. Public perceptions and definitions of criminal behavior thus have implications for both the enactment and enforcement of criminal laws.[56]

The present study vividly points to changing ideas and tolerance on the part of the public concerning the range of permissible behavior in society. When compared to popular conceptions of public order deviant behavior, a "cultural lag" is found to exist in the law. In the absence of substantive social grounding and public support for the legal status of public order crimes, the effectiveness of enacted legal norms appears questionable. In order to be effective as social control mechanisms criminal laws should agree with the major themes and cultural beliefs of a society.

The changing public designation of deviant behavior is an indication that the "moral passage" described by Gusfield (1967) is occurring with regard to public order crimes. Moral passage indicates public acceptance of a "sick" view over an "enemy

68

deviant" view and the possible approaching legitimacy of these kinds of crimes. Because such behavior is no longer viewed as threatening (i.e., enemy deviance) to established norms, moral passage reduces the effectiveness of sanctions imposed by criminal law. Public acceptance of the new moral status of public order deviant behavior may also result in changing modes of social control (for example, the substitution of "treatment" methods over imprisonment), as well as a symbolic loss in the social dominance of moral codes held by certain segments of the population (Hills, 1971).

The fact that people may respond more to their beliefs or definitions of others than to objective information does not preclude the correlation of other factors with changes in these definitions. Public notions or stereotypes of deviants are not, or assumed to be, the sole support of negative reactions to decriminalization of public order laws. The extent of the influence and effects of tangential variables on probabilities of criminalization remains a subject for future research.

The Labeling Approach

The distinctive contribution that the labeling approach makes to the study of deviant behavior resides in the relativity of social definitions of crime. The effectiveness of the linear model to measure and assess the definitional dimension is not completely unqualified, however. Alternate statistical models might also be supported by these same data. Yet the linear relationship and direction empirically established between the knowledge contingency, or the intensity with which certain types of beliefs are held, and the formal (legal) designation of deviant, indicates goodness of fit for hypotheses derived from the model. When tested, these hypotheses were favored rather than rejected by sample members in the majority of cases.

The operational definitions of knowledge contingency and punishment contingency are reasonable indicators of the variables being measured. Though clearly in the latter case, specifically in reference to narcotic and homosexual crimes, conceptual reinforcement and clarification through repeated empirical studies would be desirable. The magnitude of the partial r's and the beta regression coefficients in the case of the narcotic punishment contingency are particularly illustrative. In this example of deviant behavior the multiple R is much smaller than the largest total independent correlation with the dependent variable. This fact strongly alludes to the possibility of multicollinearity and attentuation due to interaction effects, suggesting that the relationship between the punishment contingency and independent variables may be multiplicative or nonadditive in nature.

We have in effect derived two separate measures, one for each dependent variable. Comparisons were subsequently made on the proportion and magnitude of variance each measure explained. Path analysis is suggested as an alternative measure and multiplicative model that would better control for nonadditivity or statistical interaction (Blalock, 1969; 1964). This model would concommitantly measure the joint effects of legal decriminalization and the punishment contingency as dichotomous dependent variables and perhaps provide a better fit to the data. In addition, the need for refinement of the punishment contingency as a basic conceptual construct in labeling theory remains substantial. Moreover, improvement over the weakness of low item internal consistency (content validity) in the punishment contingency measuring instrument might also be an important factor in the final analysis and facilitate greater accuracy in measurement at this stage of research design.

Concentration on the development of construct validity appears to be essential in further validation of labeling theory. The critical components of the punishment contingency cannot be effectively isolated for further testing without it. A number of hypotheses have been generated in the present study pointing to a clear relation of construct validity to labeling theory. Among these variables are age, socio-economic status and the knowledge contingency. At a minimum, these variables establish the required network of relationships essential for integrating independent variables into a general labeling framework. These indicators also provide channels by which the validity of labeling postulates can systematically be assessed, either in terms of existing evidence, as in the present study, or in terms of potential alternative conceptualizations in future research efforts.

The labeling model has provided a theoretical framework for the analysis of both the creation of criminal definitions and the response of the individual to the application of these definitions (Quinney, 1971). Operational definitions utilized in the study were also confirmed at the concrete level (Reynolds, 1971) and meet the predictive power criterion of effectiveness and testability for theory construction (Gibbs, 1972).

Since the knowledge contingency in deviance perception is viewed as the most crucial variable in the study, it would be reasonable to conclude its significance in the present research outcome approximates reality to some degree. Labeling premises are thus in line with social reality and provide a clear contrast to other traditions in deviance theory. Clearly, the changing nature of public attitudes toward the criminal law, as reflected in the present study, is an indication that categories of crime may not be immutable (Schur, 1969).

The Question of Legal Decriminalization

The question of what kinds of behavior should be defined as criminal receives interpretive and declarative response in the study. Three kinds of individual behavior (abortion, prostitution, and homosexuality) severely condemned in the criminal law and by concepts of public morality have achieved wide toleration and acceptance by society. The extent of public acceptance extends to the extent of deleting these crimes from legal statutes. This points sharply to evidence of an "overcriminalization" problem. As Packer (1968)364) indicates:

> Crime is a sociopolitical artifact, not a natural phenomenon.
> We can have as much or as little as we please, depending on what
> we choose to count as criminal. Only when this basic fact is
> understood can we begin to deal rationally with the problem of
> applying relevant criteria for proper uses of the (criminal)
> sanction.

In full measure, persons are not really criminals unless a law defines their behavior as a crime (Roby, 1969). It is in this context that many writers contend that nothing should be punished by the law that does not lie beyond the limits of tolerance. Use of the criminal law to enforce morals invokes a heavy and unnecessary social cost (Kadish, 1967; Packer, 1968; Devlin, 1969).[57] When considering future developments of the criminal law, some legal theorists predict that contractions or withdrawals of criminal sanctions are to be anticipated. This has special relevance for public order type crimes (Allen, 1969).

The probability that criminal definitions will be formulated or decriminalized is also contingent upon other factors. Changes in social conditions, for example, may in turn create a need for legal change (Hall, 1952; Chambliss, 1964). Ultimately the resolvement of problems of overcriminalization may call for adjustments in the definition and proportions of behaviors defined as criminal.[58] Such resolvement contemplates that public order crimes would be removed from the criminal justice system entirely and placed within a treatment system.

Proponents of a labeling point of view argue that a change in legal definitions of deviants would take the profit out of labeling.[59] Because people would as a result become more tolerant, they would be less likely to label certain behaviors as problematic. A general model that incorporates the probability of change in future orientations is presented below as a modified version of Wilkin's (1964:90) feedback system:

More tolerance leads to $\longrightarrow$

less acts being defined as crimes

leads to $\longrightarrow$

less action against criminals

leads to $\longrightarrow$

less alienation of deviants

leads to $\longrightarrow$

less crime by deviant groups

leads to $\longrightarrow$

more tolerance of deviants by conforming groups

and round again _____ ↑

It is often a mistaken assumption, however, that once a problem is diagnosed constructive measures will[60] or can be taken.[61]

Geis (1972:261) has aptly summarized the consequences for society of increased toleration of deviance:

> The most effecacious method of dealing with deviancy is to
> ignore, to the furthest point of our tolerance, those items
> which we find offensive. Such response is predicated upon the
> assumptions that there exists in our society a core of values
> which exert enough appeal to win over the deviant ultimately,
> or at least to keep him within the society in terms of other
> aspects of his behavior, provided that he has not been irresolu-
> tely shut off from conforment living . . . . Concomitant with
> such tolerance is an attitude that stresses those kinds of traits
> and behavior which it is desired to elicit and to perpetuate.

Limitations of the Study and Suggestions for Future Research

The present work is a crucial but preliminary analysis of labeling hypotheses.
Additional research is necessary before important sociological questions involving the
relativity of social definitions and construction of crime can be finally answered.
Other kinds of public order crimes, for example, stand in need of empirical testing.
When diverse but related crimes (e.g., public drunkenness, exhibitionism, etc.) are
taken into consideration, the applicability of labeling principles and assumptions may
prove negligible and therefore unwarranted.

Furthermore, more research engaging larger samples and populations is needed.
Investigation of a larger number and more varied assortment of communities, both
homogeneous and heterogeneous, would permit a more conclusive test of labeling propositions.

The most critical conceptions of crime, omitted in the present study, are
those held by the more powerful segments of society (Quinney, 1970b; Liazos, 1973).
Information on the criminal definitions held by segments of society that have the

power to shape the formulation, enforcement and administration of criminal law appear most crucial to the development and integration of labeling empirical generalizations. As a critical "social audience" the agents of social control are also among the most significant of the direct reactors and labelers of deviants, for they implement criminal definitions in ongoing social action and through institutionalized procedures (Schur, 1969b). Labeling research emphasis should therefore shift in the direction of inquiry into social reactions of special interest groups (e.g., lawyers) and authorized, legally empowered authorities (e.g., police, city officials, legislators, judges, prosecutors, etc.) to determine the adequacy and comprehensiveness of labeling propositions.

This study examined questions dealing with public tendencies or predispositions toward modification of criminal laws rather than the observation of actual behavior (e.g., voting). In reiteration, the position taken by research respondents toward removal of legal statutes involving public order criminals and thus "behavior", would be considerably enhanced by the formal commitment of casting a ballot for such legal change in a public referendum or election.[62]

Finally, an important and significant variable in relation to legal decriminalization and labeling has emerged in the study. Secularized religious values of respondents were found to culminate in greater tolerance for public order deviants. Evidence is accumulating which makes illusory the assumption of a basic homogeneity in value consensus in a community with respect to the issues of criminal law content and legal decriminalization (see, for example, Cohen, et al., 1958:194-195). The role of social values in the designation and definition of criminal behavior may ultimately prove to be the most rewarding analysis in terms of contributing to the generation of more contingent theoretical explanations of public order deviant behavior and deviant behavior in general.

Chapter 1:

1. The labeling theory of deviance is rooted in the symbolic interactionist per-
    spective of George Herbert Mead (1934), Alfred Schutz (1962), and other Chicago
    sociologists. According to Mead, man is a social being whose consciousness and
    personality emerge within the context of the social process. Actually Mead
    (1918) introduced the idea of stigma and the process and effects of labeling a
    person a deviant as social response and moral revulsion to law-breaking behavior.
    For an overview of contemporary works on symbolic interactionism, see Hillman
    (1973).

2. Emphasis of the "new" perspective in deviance is on the social reality of law
    (Hall, 1963:69-88). Some of the more important analyses from this perspective
    concern theft (Hall, 1952); prohibition of alcohol (Gusfield, 1963); vagrancy
    statutes (Chambliss, 1969); sexual psychopath laws (Sutherland, 1950); marijuana
    legislation (Becker, 1963); opiate laws (Lindesmith, 1965); and bureaucracy and
    social control (Skolnick and Woodworth, 1970).

3. For an excellent overview of trends in the sociology of law in America, see
    Skolnick (1965)4-39).

4. Until recently American criminologists had largely neglected the area of law as
    a focus of concern. Schur (1968:3-16) explains this as due primarily to the
    belief that law is a static body of pronouncements. The realization that law is
    always an outcome of social processes has brought attention of the criminologists
    to the area (Reasons, 1973).

5. As Schur (1968:155) argues, if the labeling approach in deviance is adopted,
    "then the 'audience' of reactors, rather than the deviating individual, becomes
    the crucial object of research . . . . Just as societal reaction 'cause'
    deviance, so also sociolegal reactions (or 'criminalization' of certain kinds of
    deviance) in a sense cause criminal behavior or at least shape problems of crime.
    . . . Today sociologists are . . . asking "why does society label X behavior a
    crime . . . and what are the social consequences, particularly in terms of
    development of criminal self-images and role commitments, of attaching this label
    to X behavior." (Emphasis added.)

6. Although a recent Supreme Court ruling prevents state interference in any abor-
    tion decision between a woman patient and her doctor during the first three
    months of pregnancy, the abortion controversy has not ended; as recently pro-
    posed bills in some state legislatures (e.g., New York State) demonstrate, the
    issue is still being debated. The question raised in the present study is what
    role should law play in determining the outcome of the conflict?

7. The sampled population is taken from the state of Idaho, which is unquestionably
    one of the most rural in the nation in terms of population density. Population
    in the state was 698,350 in 1970 (Idaho Department of Health, 1971).

8. The test of labeling theoretical hypotheses should be better fitted to a more
    homogeneous community according to Durkheim (1933). In homogeneous societies
    where solidarity arises from similarity of members, those violating group norms
    are strongly rejected. In contrast, in heterogeneous societies, where

solidarity arises from the interdependence of functionally-differentiated persons through the division of labor, there is more tolerance of deviants and milder sanctions are employed (Linsky, 1971:307).

9. A number of studies evolving around the subject of public order crimes have been conducted in urban areas but have not been directly concerned with ranking less urban respondents. In the Report of the Commission on Population Growth and the American Future (1972), for example, a national sample was polled about their attitudes on abortion; CBS sampled a national audience in 1969 on similar matters; Psychology Today (1969) surveyed a national sample of over 8,000 respondents, plus a control group of 526 of their subscribers. A very large majority of the respondents did not regard drug addiction, alcoholism, prostitution or homosexuality as criminal behavior to be punished.

10. There are many kinds of public order type crimes, unexplored in the present study, such as disorderly conduct, traffic offenses, vagrancy, public drunkenness, exhibitionism, pornography, and gambling.

11. The final report of the Annual Chief Justice Earl Warren Conference on Advocacy in the U.S. (1972) stated in their conclusions that the criminal justice system should decriminalize "behavior which does not involve (a) the threat of the use of force against another person or persons, (b) fraud, (c) wanton destruction of property, or (d) violent attacks against the government." Such advocacy for criminal law reform is not without qualification, however. "The decriminalization of offenses does not imply approval of such behavior or that society should ignore it. It recognizes that the criminal law and its agencies are inappropriate, often even exacerbating, to such behavior, and that what is required instead is a concurrent enlargement of available community resources in medicine, public health vocational training, education, welfare and family counselling" (1972:10).

12. Abortion laws in Idaho are only relatively modified after the Supreme Court decision in January, 1973. Abortion Law #1184 reads: Every person who, except as permitted by this act, provides, supplies or administers any medicine, drug or substance to any woman or uses or employs any instrument or other means whatever upon any then pregnant woman with intent thereby to produce an abortion shall be guilty of a felony and shall be imprisoned in the state prison for not less than two and not more than five years (Section 4). Abortions are lawful, however, if performed in a hospital under the care of a physician.

13. A new attitude toward more liberalized modifications in public order criminal laws also seems to have emerged. Policy statements in 1955 from the American Law Institute (Model Penal Code), American Civil Liberties, and in 1970 from the National Council on Crime and Delinquency, all urge reform of these laws. In the Comprehensive Drug Abuse Prevention and Control Act of 1970 (84 Statute 1236, codified in sections 2142, U.S.C.) Congress changed possession of marijuana for personal use from a felony to a misdemeanor; and the National Commission on Marijuana and Drug Abuse in 1972 recommended that possession of marijuana for personal use should no longer be a federal or state offense. Illinois has also legalized homosexuality between consenting adults; Connecticut has legalized most consenting sexual acts except adultery, bestiality and necrophilia (Revised Penal Code, October, 1971) between consenting adults. A number of other states have more liberal legislation under review.

14. A hazy boundary exists between deviance and social change. Sometimes social change represents individual deviation that has "succeeded," or become organized

and politically effective; for example, in political action groups that actively "lobby" for changes in the legislation governing their behavior (see Turk, 1966; and Schur, 1971 for a more detailed discussion of this point).

Chapter 2:

15. It is not really the case that labeling theory attributes all deviant outcomes to variations in processing. Rather this perspective emphasizes the importance of "process" as a consequential feature leading to at least some types of deviant responses (Schur, 1969:312-313).

16. For an exceptional theoretically oriented work that attempts to codify and inter-relate processes which shape the identities and behavioral patterns of individuals from a symbolic interactionism frame of reference, see Lofland (1969).

17. For an excellent discussion of these polls and the characteristics of the research conducted on public order criminals, see Geiss, 1971.

18. Two important studies depart from this general orientation. Roby (1969) studied the political process, formulation and enforcement of the 1965 New York State Penal Law on Prostitution. The existence of the law was contingent upon small, interest groups who exercised power over different sections of the law. Duster (1970) researched personal viewpoints of institutionalized narcotic addicts in California rehabilitation center and attributed "failure" in rehabilitation as due to societal stigmatization.

19. Bordua (1967:149-163), for example, makes the following comment about labeling theory's conception of the deviant: "It assumes an essentially empty organism or at least one with little or no autonomous capacity to determine conduct. The process of developing deviance seems all societal response and no deviant stimulus."

20. Although many assume that Becker has taken a completely relativistic position and defines deviance as unrelated to the act, this is not quite so. Becker (1963:14) states: ". . . in short, whether a given act is deviant or not depends in part (emphasis mine) on the nature of the act (that is whether or not it violates some rule) and in part on what other people do about it."

21. By far one of the most severe critics of the labeling position to date is Hagan (1973b) who provides us with a caustic review of major works in the labeling tradition, including those of Sutherland, Lemert, Becker, Goffman, and others. The thrust of Hagan's critique nevertheless departs little from those of previous labeling iconoclasts: labeling's "conceptualization is general in the extreme"; it lacks "clear" empirical referents, and so forth (Hagan, 1973b: 389).

Chapter 3:

22. This hypothesis depends heavily on the belief that social relations are "constructed", that reality is defined and interpreted before it becomes meaningful. This is a way of saying that we act in terms of the meanings attributed to events rather than to objective events (Nettler, 1974:202). How the public responds to public order crimes is therefore a function of the way society has categorized this type of crime and criminal.

23. Public order criminals are identified in a complete sense through a particular label which generates "total identity" vis-a-vis community reaction to him. For example, the female publicly "known" in the community to be a prostitute is known to that community as a totally identified person, regardless to how similar she is in every other way to the next person (Duster, 1970). Such persons usually undergo the "identity degradation ceremony" if apprehended (Garfinkel, 1956).

24. Simmons' Work (1969) is of course exceptional to this trend.

25. An exhaustive review of such literature is not intended here. For more expanded descriptions, see Bell (1971); Geis (1971); Humphreys (1970); Lindesmith (1940); Leznoff (1956); and The National Commission of Marijuana and Drug Abuse (1973).

26. For an excellent discussion on the myth of the "sex offender", see Tappan (1955: 7-12).

27. The lethal character of heroin use is not thereby minimized. Death and debilitating diseases such as tetanus and Serum hepatitis are known to occur with frequent use of the drug.

28. See Reasons (1971) for an excellent analytical application of this thesis to contemporary social problems.

29. Schur (1961a, 1961b, 1962) in cross-cultural comparisons on drug addiction, notes that a large proportion of British addicts come from the middle and upper middle classes and from the medical and related occupations. See also Larimore and Brill (1960).

30. See also Nyswander (1965:60) for discussion of the drug addict as patient.

31. Labels are in effect a "vote" for a social world and a social view of reality. While this study represents a "position" taken by research respondents toward removal of legal statutes involving public order criminals and thus "behavior", the act of casting a ballot, say in a referendum, represents a considerably more formal commitment to a position.

32. Social scientists have engaged in considerable debate over the interpretation of empirical findings regarding the rural-urban continuum. For an excellent discussion of the pros and cons of the argument, see Beers, 1953; and Haer, 1952; also Dewey, 1960.

33. The Bureau of the Census in 1960 delineated 212 Standard Metropolitan Statistical Areas (SMSA'S) based on detailed sets of criteria (see Geist and Fava, 1964). Only one such SMSA exists in the state of Idaho (at Boise). The next closest Metropolitan Area is Spokane, Washington, contiguous to the Northwestern part of Idaho. A rural community is defined as having less than 2,500 inhabitants.

34. By orthodox is meant those denominations which more closely adhere to traditional American religious doctrinal tenets and liturgy. According to Lenski (1961), Protestants are more orthodox than Catholics and other religious groups.

Chapter 4:

35. A complete description of sampling procedures is found in Appendix A. The

comparison of the sample to the population from which it was drawn is based upon the 1970 Bureau of Census population characteristics.

36. Appreciation is extended to Don Gibbons for provision of the questionnaire materials used in this study.

37. See Appendix C for the instrument used in collecting the data.

38. After Clayton (1973:42), the equation used to compute content validity is:
$$\frac{(av.r)\ (n)}{(av.r)\ (n)\ +\ (-av.r)}.$$

38. According to the Idaho Criminal Code, homosexuality in Idaho is considered a crime against nature punishable by not less than 5 years imprisonment (#18-6605); possession of any drug or narcotic is a misdemeanor (#37-2732)*; to manufacture or deliver a controlled substance which is a narcotic may result in a sentence of not more than 15 years or $25,000 fine, or both for violators. Probation is a minimum penalty under present legal guidelines (#37-2705).
*Note: In April of this year possession of marijuana in the amount of three ounces became a felony in Idaho.

40. In knowledge of deviance type questions respondents are also compared with popular myths and misconceptions of deviants and on more accurate information founded on sociological research (see, for example, Bell, 1971 and Reiss, 1965).

41. Forty percent (N = 100) of respondents omitted listing their occupations on the questionnaire.

42. The multiple regression design must meet the following conditions: "(1) k independent interval level variables where $k \geq 1$. These variables are assumed to be measured without error at the preset values selected by the experimenter. When the experiment consists of only one independent variable (k - 1), then the results of this approach are identical to those from a simple bivariate correlation or regression design. (2) Each subject in the sample is observed on all k + 1 variables (including the dependent variable y)" (Gray, 1972:35).

43. By setting up the variables in this fashion minus correlations will equal positive relations for urban, male and Protestant nominal variables.

44. Some of the independent variables are combined and therefore some S_i may be the product of scores on two variables. In this case such terms would also be considered interactions (Carlson, 1972). Although this approach to interaction is not often used in the social sciences, it is perfectly legitimate mathematically (Mendenhall, 1968). Interaction terms combined in the present study are education and income, age and knowledge, and education and knowledge.

Chapter 5:

45. These findings provide a platform of agreement for recent Supreme Court decisions liberalizing abortion laws.

46. For a more detailed breakdown and cross tabulation of study results, see Appendix B.

47. The beta coefficients are especially useful in determining the relative importance

in affecting or predicting variation in the dependent variable after effects of all other variables have been eliminated. Regression coefficients measure the slope of the regression line; that is, they show the average number of units increase or decrease of a specified unit of the dependent variable which occurs with each increase or decrease of a specified unit of the independent variable (Lander, 1954).

48. Type 1 error is failure to reject the null hypothesis that b/ is zero when in fact the null hypothesis is false. Type 2 error is rejecting the null hypothesis that b/ is zero when in fact the null hypothesis is true.

49. Methodological problems in the socio-economic indice, however, may pose limitations to the study. Previous research has shown that the construction of indices of socio-economic status by averaging up in some manner several status variables are seriously deficient in characterizing the social status of a significant majority of the population (Lenski, 1954:405-13).

50. Means and standard deviations for all multiple correlations are also provided in Appendix B.

51. It should be noted that individuals are responding to the user of narcotics rather than to the pusher of narcotics (see Appendix C for a description of the fictional case history involved.)

52. High scores for the punishment contingency are equated with treatment alternatives and low scores indicate punishment.

53. According to Hamblin (no date), the average amount of explained variance in correlation studies in sociology is about 12 percent.

54. These conclusions on socio-economic status are not inconsistent with past studies on labeling applications. Previous research on psychological disorders, for example, suggests that low status groups may view a wider range of behavior as "normal" or "tolerable" than upper status groups but that once a label has been applied, they may actually be less tolerant (Dohrenwend and Chin-Shong, 1967: 447-453).

Chapter 6:

55. Toleration for these crimes does not imply approval of the behavior in question.

56. Blumstein and Cohen (1973:198-207) claim that a shift in attitudes and changes in social definitions are already being reflected in arrest data. The number of arrests for most public order crimes, for example, has decreased over the last five years. Legal restrictions on narcotic abuse, favored by the majority in this study, are also reflected in arrest statistics. The number of arrests for violation of narcotic and drug laws increased 575 percent over the last five years.

57. Reasons (1973:472-473) has also been a consistent critic of the "overcriminalization" of our laws and calls for a "demystification" of the law and legal institutions, especially with reference to victimless crimes.

58. For obvious reasons this does not apply to the crime of narcotic use. Many object that the withdrawal of the criminal sanction for narcotics would signify

approval of use and encourage more consumption of the drug. The fact that this deviant activity has become a political issue, however, is a sign to some that its moral status is at stake and that legitimacy is possible (Gusfield, 1967: 188).

59. Sykes (1972:408) captures the essence of this perspective in the statement: "man has the inalienable right to go to hell in his own fashion."

60. As Schur (1965:175) suggests, it seems apparent that opponents of legal reformation of public order crimes have made it a point to neglect objective facts or information about the relatively harmless aspects of public order deviance-- "which would after all considerably weaken their arguments."

61. Decriminalization of public order crimes, for example, may not be equally favored by various legal agents of society (e.g., legislators, police, prosecutors, judges), and any successful program of legal changes involves, and is dependent upon these persons to provide direction to present and future policies and practices in this area.

62. Study emphasis on predispositions to act rather than observable behavior may not pose a serious problem if previous research is any indication. Albrecht, et al. (1972), for example, studied the predisposition to act as a predictor of behavior and the overt act jointly in estimating the propensity of college students to legalize marijuana and found that verbal behavior alone was the most important factor in determining behavior.

REFERENCES

Akers, Ronald L.
 1968 "Problems in the Sociology of Deviance: Social Definitions and Behavior," Social Forces, 46 (June):455-465.

Albrecht, S., M. DeFleur and L. Warner
 1972 "Attitude-Behavior Relationships: A Reexamination of the Postulate of Contingent Consistency," Pacific Sociological Review, 15, 2 (April): 149-168.

Allen, Francis A.
 1964 The Borderline of Criminal Justice; Essays in Law and Criminology. Chicago: The University of Chicago Press.

Alston, Jon P. and K. Imogene Dean
 1972 "Socioeconomic Factors Associated with Attitudes toward Welfare Recipients and the Causes of Poverty," Social Service Review, 46, 1 (January):1-11.

Anderson, H. D. and Percy Davidson
 1940 Occupational Trends in the United States. Stanford: Stanford University Press.

Andreas, Carol
 1971 Sex and Caste in America. Englewood Cliffs: Prentice-Hall, Inc.

Ashley, Richard
 1972 Heroin: The Myths and the Facts. New York: St. Martin's Press.

Becker, Howard
 1963 Outsiders. New York: Free Press.

Beers, Howard A.
 1953 "Rural-Urban Differences: Some Evidence from Public Opinion Polls," Rural Sociology, 18 (March):1-11.

Bell, Robert
 1971 Social Deviance. Homewood: Dorsey Press.

Bittner, E.
 1972 "Police Discretion in Emergency Apprehension of Mentally Ill Persons." In Wm. J. Filstead (ed.) An Introduction to Deviance: Readings in the Process of Making Deviants. Chicago: Markham.

Blalock, Hubert M., Jr.
 1964 Causal Inferences in Nonexperimental Research. New York: W. W. Norton and Company, Inc.

 1969 Theory Construction from Verbal to Mathematical Formulations. Englewood Cliffs: Prentice-Hall, Inc.

 1972 Social Statistics. New York: McGraw-Hill, Inc.

Brakel, Samuel J. and Galen R. South
    1969   "Diversion from the Criminal Process in the Rural Community," The
               American Criminal Law Quarterly, 7, 3 (Spring):124-125.

Brown, R. R. and J. E. Partington
    1942   "The Intelligence of the Narcotic Drug Addict," Journal of General
               Psychology, 26 (January):175-179.

Burgess, Ernest W.
    1952   "Family Living in the Later Decades," The Annals of the American
               Academy of Political and Social Science:279.

Burkett, Steven R.
    1972   "Self-Other Systems and Deviant Career Patterns," Pacific Sociological
               Review, 15, 2 (April):169.

Bustamante, Jorge A.
    1972   "The 'Wetback' as Deviant: An Application of Labeling Theory,"
               American Journal of Sociology, 77, 4 (January):706-718.

Carlson, John
    1972   A Sociological Analysis of Factors Affecting Recreational Behavior.
               Unpublished Doctoral Dissertation. Pullman: Washington State
               University.

Chambliss, William J.
    1964   "A Sociological Analysis of the Law of Vagrancy," Social Problems, 12
               (Summer):67-77.

    1969   Crime and the Legal Process. New York: McGraw-Hill Book Company.

Chapman, Dennis
    1968   Sociology and the Stereotype of the Criminal. London: Tavistock
               Publications.

Chiricos, Theodore G. and Phillip D. Jackson
    1972   "Inequality in the Imposition of a Criminal Label," Social Problems, 19,
               4 (Spring):553-572.

Cicourel, Aaron V.
    1968   The Social Organization of Juvenile Justice. New York: Wiley and
               Sons, Inc.

Clayton, S. C.
    1973   The Commitment Concept and an Application to Conventional Values.
               Unpublished Doctoral Dissertation. Pullman: Washington State University.

Clinard, Marshall B.
    1964   "The Relationship of Urbanization and Urbanism to Criminal Behavior."
               In E. W. Burgess (ed.) Contributions to Urban Sociology. Chicago:
               University of Chicago Press.

    1968   Sociology of Deviant Behavior. 3rd ed. New York: Holt, Rinehart and
               Winston, Publishers.

    1974   Sociology of Deviant Behavior. 4th ed. New York: Holt, Rinehart and

Winston, Inc.

Clinard, Marshall B. and Richard Quinney
    1973   Criminal Behavior Systems, A Typology. 2nd ed. New York: Holt, Rinehart and Winston, Inc.

Cohen, Albert K. and James F. Short, Jr.
    1971   "Crime and Juvenile Delinquency." In Robert K. Merton and R. Nisbet (eds.) Contemporary Social Problems. 3rd ed. New York: Harcourt Brace Jovanovich.

Cohen, Julius, Reginald A. H. Robson and Allan Bates
    1958   Parental Authority: The Community and the Law. New Brunswick: Rutgers University Press.

Cronbach, L. J. and P. E. Meehl
    1955   "Construct Validity in Psychological Tests," Psychological Bulletin, 52:281-302.

Day, Frank D.
    1964   Criminal Law and Society. Springfield: Charles C. Thomas, Publishers.

Devlin, Patrick
    1969   The Enforcement of Morals. London: Oxford University Press.

Dewey, Richard
    1960   "The Rural-Urban Continuum: Real but Relatively Unimportant," American Journal of Sociology, 66, 1 (August):60-65.

Dicey, A. F.
    1905   Lectures on the Relation Between Law and Public Opinion in England During the Nineteenth Century. London: Macmillan and Company, pp. 1-16.

Dinkel, Robert M.
    1944   "Attitudes of Children Toward Supporting Aged Parents," American Sociological Review, 9 (April):71-83.

Cohrenwend, Bruce P. and Edwin Chi-Shong
    1967   "Social Status and Attitudes Toward Psychological Disorder: The Problem of Tolerance of Deviance," American Sociological Review, 32, 3 (June): 417-432.

Douglas, Jack D.
    1971   American Social Order; Social Rules in a Pluralistic Society. New York: Free Press.

Duncan, Otis and Peter Blau
    1967   The American Occupational Structure in the United States. New York: John Wiley and Sons, Inc.

Durkheim, Emile
    1933   Division of Labor in Society. Glencoe: Free Press. George Simpson, translator.

    1966   The Rules of the Sociological Method. 8th ed. (George E. G. Catlin, ed. Translated by S. A. Solovay and J. H. Mueller.) New York: Free Press.

Duster, Troy
1970   The Legislation of Morality: Law, Drugs and Moral Judgement. New York: Free Press.

Eisner, Victor
1969   The Delinquency Label: The Epidemiology of Juvenile Delinquency. New York: Random House.

Erikson, Kai
1962   "Notes on the Sociology of Deviance," Social Problems, 9 (Spring):307-314.

1966   Wayward Puritans. New York: Wiley and Sons, Inc.

Evans, William M. (ed.)
1962   Law and Society. New York: Free Press.

Faust, Frederic L.
1973   "Delinquency Labeling; Its Consequences and Implications," Crime and Delinquency, 19, 1 (January):41-48.

Feldman, Saul and Gerald Thieban
1972   Life Styles: Diversity in American Society. Boston: Little, Brown and Company.

Fischer, Claude S.
1971   "A Research Note on Urbanism and Tolerance," American Journal of Sociology, 76, 5 (March):847-856.

Fisher, Sethard
1972   "Stigma and Deviant Careers in School," Social Problems, 20, 1 (Summer): 78-84.

Foster, Jack D., Simon Dinitz and Walter C. Reckless
1972   "Perceptions of Stigma Following Public Intervention for Delinquent Behavior," Social Problems, 20, 2 (Fall):202-209.

Friedmann, W.
1972   Law in a Changing Society. 2nd ed. New York: Columbia University Press.

Gardiner, John A.
1967   "Public Attitudes Toward Gambling and Corruptions," Annals of the American Academy of Political and Social Science, 374 (November):123-134.

Garfinkel, Harold
1956   "Conditions of Successful Degradation Ceremonies," American Journal of Sociology, 61:420-24.

Gebhard, Paul H., J. H. Gagnon, W. B. Promerely and C. V. Christenson
1969   Sex Offenders. New York: Harper and Row.

Geis, Gilbert
1972   Not the Laws Business? An Examination of Homosexuality, Abortion, Prostitution, Narcotics, and Gambling in the United States.

Washington, D.C., National Institute of Mental Health, Center for Studies of Crime and Delinquency.

Geist, Noel and Sylvia Fava
1964   Urban Society. 5th ed. New York: Thomas Y. Crowell Company.

Gibbons, Don C.
1963   "Who Knows What About Corrections?", Crime and Delinquency, 9 (April): 137-144.

1969   "Crime and Punishment: A Study in Social Attitudes," Social Forces, 47, 4 (June):391-97.

1971   "Observations on the Study of Crime Causation," American Journal of Sociology, 77, 2 (September):262-278.

1973   Society, Crime, and Criminal Careers. 2nd ed. Englewood Cliffs: Prentice-Hall, Inc.

Gibbons, Don C. and Joseph F. Jones
1971   "Some Critical Notes on Current Definitions of Deviance," Pacific Sociological Review, 14, 1 (January):20-37.

Gibbs, Jack P.
1966a   "Conceptions of Deviant Behavior," Pacific Sociological Review, (Spring); 9-14.

1966b   "Crime and the Sociology of Law," American Sociological Review, 51, 1 (October):23-33.

1972a   "Issues in Defining Deviant Behavior." In Scott, Robert A. and Jack D. Douglas (eds.) Theoretical Perspectives on Deviance. New York: Basic Books, Inc.

1972b   "Social Control," Warner Modular Publications, Module 1:1-17.

1972c   Sociological Theory Construction. Hinsdale: The Dryden Press, Inc.

Gilbert, G. M.
1958   "Crime and Punishment: An Exploratory Comparison of Public, Criminal and Penological Attitudes," Mental Hygiene, 42, 1 (October):550-557.

Glaser, Daniel
1967   "National Goals and Indicators for the Reduction of Crime and Delinquency," The Annals of the American Academy of Political and Social Science, 1 (May):104-126.

1971   "Criminology and Public Policy," The American Sociologist, 6 (Supplementary Issue):30-37.

Glenn, Norval D. and John P. Alston
1968   "Cultural Distances Among Occupational Categories," American Sociological Review, 33 (June):365-482.

Glock, Charles Y. and Rodney Stark
1969   Christian Beliefs and Anti-Semitism. New York: Harper and Row

Publishers.

Glueck, Sheldon and Eleanor
    1962   Family Environment and Delinquency. Boston: Houghton Mifflin.

Goffman, Erving
    1963   Stigma: Notes on the Management of Spoiled Identity. Englewood Cliffs:
                Prentice-Hall, Inc.

Goldman, Nathan
    1969   "Social Breakdown," The Annals of the American Academy of Political and
                Social Science (March).

Gould, Leroy C.
    1969   "Who Defines Delinquency: A Comparison of Self-Reported and Officially-
                Reported Indices of Delinquency for Three Racial Groups," Social
                Problems, 16 (Winter):325-336.

Gouldner, Alvin W.
    1968   "The Sociologist as Partisan," The American Sociologist, 3 (May):103-116.

Gove, W. R.
    1970   "Societal Reaction as an Explanation of Mental Illness: An Evaluation,"
                American Sociological Review, 35 (October):873-84.

Gray, Louis N.
    1972   Multiple Regression Design. Unpublished Monograph. Pullman:
                Washington State University, Department of Sociology.

Gusfield, Joseph
    1967   "Moral Passage: The Symbolic Process in Public Designation of Deviance,"
                Social Problems, 15 (Fall):175-188.

    1972   "Prohibition: The Impact of Political Utopianism." In John Braeman
                (ed.) The 1920's Revisited. Columbus: Ohio State University Press.

Hackler, James C.
    1970   "Testing of a Causal Model of Delinquency," Sociological Quarterly, 11
                (Fall):511-522.

Haer, John L.
    1952   "Conservatism-Radicalism and the Rural-Urban Continuum," Rural Sociology,
                17 (December):343-47.

Hagan, John
    1973a   "Labeling and Deviance: A Case Study in the 'Sociology of the Inter-
                esting'," Social Problems, 20, 4 (Spring):447-458.

    1973b   "Conceptual Deficiencies of an Interactionist Perspective in Deviance,"
                Criminology, 11, 3 (November):383-404.

Hamblin, Robert L.
    1968   "Apparent Versus Underlying Relationships," Report Number 1, Unpublished
                Monograph. St. Louis: Washington University.

    No Date Ratio Measurement and Sociological Theory: A Critical Analysis.

87

Unpublished Monograph. St. Louis: Washington University.

Harlow, Eleanor
    1971   Diversion from the Criminal Justice System. National Institute of
            Mental Health, Center for Studies of Crime and Delinquency. Public
            Health Service Publication No. 2129.

Harmsworth, Harry C.
    1954   A Survey of the Alcohol and Narcotics Problem in Idaho. Moscow:
            University of Idaho.

Hillman, John (ed.)
    1973   "Symbolic Interactionism: Special Issue," Catalyst, 7 (Winter).

Hills, Stuart L.
    1971   Crime, Power, and Morality. The Criminal Law Process in the United
            States. Scranton: Chandler Publishers.

Hirschi, Travis
    1969   Causes of Delinquency. California: University of California Press.

Hoffman, Martin
    1968   The Gay World: Male Homosexuality and the Social Question of Evil.
            New York: Bantam.

Hooker, E.
    1957   "The Adjustment of the Male Overt Homosexual," Journal of Projective
            Techniques, 22:33-54.

    1966   "The Homosexual Community." In James O. Palmer and Michael J.
            Goldstein (eds.) Perspectives in Psychopathology: Readings in Abnormal
            Psychology. New York: Oxford University Press.

Humphreys, Laud
    1970   "Tearoom Trade: Impersonal Sex in Public Places," Transaction, 7, 3
            (January):8.

Jeffery, C. R.
    1956   "The Structure of American Criminological Thinking," Journal of Criminal
            Law, Criminology, and Police Science, (January-February):658-72.

    1970   "Social Change and Criminal Law," American Behavioral Scientist, 13, 4
            (March-April):523-530.

Jensen, Gary F.
    1972   "Delinquency and Adolescent Self-Conceptions: A Study of the Personal
            Relevance of Infraction," Social Problems, 20, 1 (Summer):84-102.

Johnson, Kenneth A. and Keith Grieneeks
    1973   "Juvenile Delinquent Recidivism in Idaho," Journal of the Idaho Academy
            of Science, 9, 2 (December):49-64.

Julian, Joseph
    1973   Social Problems. New York: Appleton-Century Crofts.

Kadish, Sanford H.
    1967   "The Crisis of Over-Criminalization," Annals of the American Academy of
               Political and Social Science, 374 (November):157-170.

Kitsuse, John I.
    1962   "Societal Reaction to Deviant Behavior: Problems of Theory and Method,"
               Social Problems, 9 (Winter):347-356.

    1964   "Societal Reaction to Deviance: Problems of Theory and Method." In H.
               Becker (ed.) The Other Side: Perspectives on Deviance. Glencoe: Free
               Press.

Kitsuse, John and Thomas Scheff
    1964   "The Societal Reaction to Deviance: Ascriptive Elements in the
               Psychiatric Screening of Mental Patients in a Midwestern State," Social
               Problems, 11 (Spring):401-413.

Klapp, Orrin E.
    1962   Heroes, Villains, and Fools. Englewood Cliffs: Prentice-Hall, Inc.

Lander, B.
    1954   Towards an Understanding of Juvenile Delinquency. New York: Columbia
               University Press.

Larimore, G. and H. Brill
    1960   "The British Narcotic System Report of Study," New York State Journal of
               Medicine, 60 (January):107-115.

Lemert, Edwin M.
    1951   Social Pathology. New York: McGraw-Hill, Inc.

    1967   Human Deviance, Social Problems, and Social Control. Englewood Cliffs:
               Prentice-Hall, Inc.

Lenski, Gerhard
    1954   "Status Crystallization: A Numerical Dimension of Social Status,"
               American Sociological Review, 19 (August):405-413.

    1961   The Religious Factor. New York: Doubleday and Company.

Lentz, William P.
    1965   "Public Stereotypes of Deviants," Social Problems, 13 (Fall): 223-232.

    1966   "Social Status and Attitudes toward Delinquency Control," Journal of
               Research in Crime and Delinquency, (July):147-54.

Leznoff, M. and W. A. Westley
    1956   "The Homosexual Community," Social Problems, 3 (April):257-263.

Liazos, Alexander
    1972   "The Poverty of the Sociology of Deviance: Nuts, Sluts, and Perverts,"
               Social Problems, 20, 1 (Summer):103-119.

Lindesmith, A. R.
    1940   "'Dope-Fiend' Mythology," Journal of Criminal Law, Criminology and
               Police Science, 31, 2:199-208.

Lindesmith, A. R.
    1965   The Addict and the Law. Bloomington: Indiana University Press.

Linsky, Arnold S.
    1970a   "Community Homogeneity and Exclusion of the Mentally Ill: Rejection Versus Consensus About Deviance," American Journal of Psychiatry, (August):160-67.

    1970b   "Who Shall Be Excluded: The Influence of Personal Attributes in Community Reaction to the Mentally Ill," Social Psychiatry, 5 (July): 166-71.

Lofland, John
    1969   Deviance and Identity. Englewood Cliffs: Prentice-Hall, Inc.

Lowry, Ritchie
    1974   Social Problems: A Critical Analysis of Theories and Public Policy. Sexington, Massachusetts: D. C. Heath and Company.

Mannheim, Hermann
    1946   Criminal Justice and Social Reconstruction. New York: Oxford University Press.

Marshall, Harvey and Ross Purdy
    1972   "Hidden Deviance and the Labeling Approach: The Case for Drinking and Driving," Social Problems, 19, 4 (Spring):541-553.

Matza, David
    1969   Becoming Deviant. Englewood Cliffs: Prentice-Hall, Inc.

McIntyre, Jennie
    1967   "Public Attitudes Toward Crime and Law Enforcement," Annals of the American Academy of Political and Social Science, 374 (November):34-46.

Mead, George H.
    1918   "The Psychology of Punitive Justice," American Journal of Sociology, 23:577-602.

    1934   Mind, Self, and Society. Chicago: University of Chicago Press.

Mendenhall
    1968   Introduction to Linear Models and the Design and Analysis of Experiments. Belmont, California: Wadsworth Publishing Company.

Morris, Terence
    1966   "The Social Toleration of Crime." In Hugh J. Klare (ed.) Changing Concepts of Crime and Its Treatment. Oxford: Pergamon Press:13-34.

Motley, Constance P.
    1973   "Law and Order and the Criminal Justice System," The Journal of Criminal Law and Criminology, 64, 3 (September):259-269.

National Commission on Marijuana and Drug Abuse. Second Report.
    1973   Drug Use in America: Problem in Perspective. Washington, D.C., U.S. Government Printing Office.

Nettler, Gwynn
     1974   Explaining Crime. New York: McGraw-Hill Book Company.

New York Times
     1970   Social Profile: USA Today. New York: Van Nostrand Reinhold Company.

Newman, Donald J.

     1957   "Public Attitudes Toward a Form of White Collar Crime," Social Problems,
               4 (January):228-232.

Nye, Ivan F.
     1958   Family Relations and Delinquent Behavior. New York: Wiley and Sons, Inc.

Nyswander, M.
     1965   The Drug Addict as a Patient. New York: Grune and Stratton.

Oppenheim, A. N.
     1966   Questionnaire Design and Attitude Measurement. New York: Basic Books,
               Inc., Publishers.

Packer, H. L.
     1968   The Limits of the Criminal Sanction. Stanford: Stanford University
               Press.

Parker, Howard A.
     1970   "Juvenile Court Actions and Public Response." In P. G. Carabedian and
               Don C. Gibbons (eds.) Becoming Delinquent. Chicago: Aldine Publishers:
               252-65.

Pattison, E. M., L. A. Bishop, and A. S. Linsky
     1968   "Changes in Public Attitudes on Narcotic Addiction," American Journal of
               Psychiatry, (August):160-67.

Payne, William D.
     1973   "Negative Labels: Passageways and Prisons," Crime and Delinquency, 19, 1
               (January):33-40.

Piliavin, I. and S. Briar
     1964   "Police Encounter with Juveniles," American Journal of Sociology, 70
               (September):206-14.

Platt, Anthony
     1969   "The Rise of the Child-Saving Movement: A Study in Social Policy and
               Correctional Reform," The Annals of the American Academy of Political
               and Social Science, 381 (January):21-38.

Poveda, Tony
     1972   "The Fear of Crime in a Small Town," Crime and Delinquency, 18, 2 (April).

Quinney, Richard
     1970a   The Problem of Crime. New York: Dodd, Mead and Company.

     1970b   The Social Reality of Crime. Boston: Little, Brown and Company.

Quinney, Richard
    1971   "Crime: Phenomenon, Problem, and Subject of Study." In Erwin O. Smigel
                (ed.) Handbook of the Study of Social Problems. Chicago: Rand McNally
                and Company:209-246.

Reasons, Charles
    1971   An Inquiry in the Sociology of Social Problems: The Drug Problem in
                Twentieth Century America. Unpublished Doctoral Dissertation. Pullman:
                Washington State University.

    1973   "The Politicizing of Crime, the Criminal and the Criminologist," The
                Journal of Criminal Law and Criminology, 64, 4 (December):471-477.

Reiss, Ira L.
    1961   "The Social Integration of Queers and Peers," Social Problems, 9, 2
                (Fall):102-119.

    1970   "Premarital Sex as Deviant Behavior: An Application of Current Approaches
                to Deviance," American Sociological Review, 35 (February):78-82.

Reynolds, P. D.
    1971   A Primer in Theory Construction. New York: The Bobbs-Merrill Company,
                Inc.

Roby, Pamela A.
    1969   "Politics and Criminal Law: Revision of the New York State Penal Law on
                Prostitution," Social Problems, 17, 1 (Summer):83-109.

Rooney, Elizabeth and Don Gibbons
    1966   "Social Reactions to 'Crimes Without Victims'," Social Problems, 15
                (Spring):400-440.

Roscoe-Pound American Trial Lawyers Foundation
    1972   A Program for Prison Reform. The Final Report. Annual Chief Justice
                Earl Warren Conference on Advocacy in the United States. (June),
                Cambridge.

Rose, Arnold and Arthur E. Prell
    1955   "Does the Punishment Fit the Crime? A Study in Social Valuation,"
                American Journal of Sociology, 61 (November):247-59.

Rubington, Earl and Martin S. Weinberg
    1968   Deviance: The Interactionist Perspective. New York: The Macmillan
                Company.

    1971   The Study of Social Problems: Five Perspectives. New York: Oxford
                University Press.

Rushing, William A.
    1971   "Individual Resources, Societal Reaction, and Hospital Commitment,"
                American Journal of Sociology, 77, 3 (November):511-525.

Scheff, Thomas J.
    1964   "The Societal Reaction to Deviance: Ascriptive Elements in the Psychi-
                atric Screening of Mental Patients in a Midwestern State," Social

Problems, 11 (Spring):401-413.

1966 Being Mentally Ill: A Sociological Theory. Chicago: Aldine Publishers.

Schott, Webster
  1967 "A 4-Million Minority Asks for Equal Rights," New York Times Magazine, (November):45A.

Schur, Edwin
  1961a "British Narcotics Policies," Journal of Criminal Law, Criminology, and Police Science, 51 (March-April):619-629.

  1961b "Drug Addiction under British Policy," Social Problems, 9, 2 (Fall): 156-166.

  1962 Narcotic Addiction in Britain and America. Bloomington: Indiana University Press.

  1965 Crimes Without Victims: Deviant Behavior and Public Policy. Englewood Cliffs: Prentice-Hall, Inc.

  1968 Law and Society: A Sociological View. New York: Random House.

  1969a Our Criminal Society: The Social and Legal Sources of Crime in America. Englewood Cliffs: Prentice-Hall, Inc.

  1969b "Reactions to Deviance: A Critical Assessment," American Journal of Sociology, 75 (November):309-322.

  1971 Labeling Deviant Behavior: Its Sociological Implications. New York: Harper and Row, Publishers.

Schutz, Alfred
  1962 Collected Papers I: The Problem of Social Reality. The Hague: Martinus Nijhoff.

Schwartz, Richard D. and Sonya Orleans
  1967 "On Legal Sanctions," University of Chicago Law Review, 34, 2 (Winter): 283-300.

Sellin, Thorsten
  1938 Culture Conflict and Crime. New York: Social Science Research Council.

Selltiz, C., M. Jahoda, M. Deutsch, and S. W. Cook
  1959 Research Methods in Social Relations. Revised One-Volume Edition.

Shoemaker, Donald, Donald R. South and Jay Lowe
  1973 "Facial Stereotypes of Deviants and Judgments of Guilt or Innocence," Social Forces, 51, 4 (June):427-433.

Simmons, Jerry L.
  1965 "Public Stereotypes of Deviants," Social Problems, 13 (Fall):223-232.

  1969 Deviants. Berekley: Glendessary.

Skolnick, Jerome

1965 "The Sociology of Law in America: Overview and Trends," Law and Society, A Supplement to the Summer Issue of Social Problems:4-39.

1966 Justice Without Trial: Law Enforcement in Democratic Society. New York: John Wiley and Sons, Inc.

Skolnick, Jerome and J. Richard Woodworth
1970 "Bureaucracy, Information, and Social Control: A Study of a Morals Detail." In R. D. Schwartz and Jerome H. Skolnick (eds.) Society and the Legal Order; Cases and Materials in the Sociology of Law. New York: Basic Books, Inc., Publishers.

Smigel, Ervin O.
1956 "Public Attitudes Toward Stealing as Related to Size of the Victim Organizations," American Sociological Review, 21 (June):320-327.

Stern, Gerald
1967 "Public Drunkenness: Crime or Health Problem?", Annals of the American Academy of Political and Social Science, 374 (November):147-156.

Stinchcombe, Arthur
1968 Construction Social Theories. New York: Harcourt, Brace and World, Inc.

Stoll, Clarice S.
1968 "Images of Man and Social Control," Social Forces, 47, 2 (December):119-126.

Sykes, Gresham M.
1972 "The Future of Criminality," American Behavioral Scientists, 15, 3 (January-February):403-419.

Taber, Merlin, Herbert C. Quay, Harold Mark and Vicki Nealey
1969 "Disease Ideology and Mental Health Research," Social Problems, 16, 3 (Winter):349-356.

Tannenbaum, Frank
1939 Crime and the Community. New York: Columbia University Press.

Tappan
1955 "Some Myths About the Sex Offender," Federal Probation, 19 (June).

Task Force Report (President's Commission)
1967 President's Commission on Law Enforcement and Administration of Justice. Task Force Report: Crime and Its Impact; An Assessment.

Trice, Harrison M. and Paul M. Roman
1970 "Delabeling, Relabeling, and Alcoholics Anonymous," Social Problems, 17, 4 (Spring):538-545.

Turk, Austin T.
1966 "Conflict and Criminality," American Sociological Review, 3 (June):338-352.

1969 Criminality and the Legal Order. Chicago: Rand McNally and Company.

U. S. Senate Committee on Labor and Public Welfare. Subcommittee on Alcoholism and Narcotics.
  1971   Marijuana and Health; A Report to the Congress from the Secretary, Department of Health, Education, and Welfare, 92 Congress, 1st Session (March):5.

Von Mering, Otto
  1968   "Cultural Values in Normal Senescence, Illness, and Death: An Essay in Comparative Gerontology," Psychiatric Communications, (January):63-73.

Weber, Max
  1958   The Protestant Ethic and the Spirit of Capitalism. Translated Talcott Parsons. New York: Charles Scribner's Sons.

Wertham, Carl
  1967   "The Function of Social Definitions in the Development of Delinquent Careers," Task Force Report: Juvenile Delinquency and Youth Crime. President's Commission on Law Enforcement and the Administration of Justice.

Wilkins, Leslie T.
  1965   Social Deviance: Social Policy, Action, and Research. Englewood Cliffs: Prentice-Hall, Inc.

  1973   "Crime and Criminal Justice at the Turn of the Century," The Annals of the American Academy of Political and Social Science, 408 (July):13-29.

Williams, Colin J. and Martin S. Weinberg
  1970   "Being Discovered: A Study of Homosexuals in the Military," Social Problems, 18, 2 (Fall):217-227.

Wiseman, Jacqueline P.
  1969   "Your Thoughts on Crime and Punishment," Psychology Today, (May):53-58.

  1970   Stations of the Lost: The Treatment of Skid Row Alcoholics. New York: Prentice-Hall, Inc.

APPENDIX A

METHODS OF DATA COLLECTION AND SAMPLE CHARACTERISTICS

The Sample

The sample was designed to give each person 18 years old and over living in a household in Lewiston an equal probability of representation in the final results. The sampling procedures conformed to established principles of probability sampling at all stages of the process; in the selection of areas for dispensing of questionnaires and in the selection of households. It should be noted, however, that the survey sample was not designed to represent the total adult population, but rather that portion of it living in households in Lewiston and Lewiston Orchards; hence certain types of places, such as mental hospitals, homes for the aged, and other similar institutions were omitted from the sample design.

The sample was drawn by a random procedure based on a cluster of housing units per city block for all voting precincts (N = 25) in Lewiston.[a] Voting precinct blocks are considered equivalent to census data block categories. The procedure resulted in three housing units per block in which one adult in each housing unit was contacted. The purpose of the inquiry was explained by the interviewer and respondents were asked to complete the questionnaire and return it by mail. If there was no response or a refusal was encountered, the interviewer moved to the adjacent house in clockwise direction.

Characteristics of the Sample

Tables A.1 through A.5 summarize the distribution of the sample according to various demographic characteristics of Lewiston. These were then compared to the

---

[A]The number of occupied housing units in Lewiston is 8,707. Source: Housing Characteristics for States, Cities, and Counties. Vol. 1, Part 14. Idaho. U. S. Department of Commerce. Social and Economic Statistics Administration. Bureau of the Census. 14.

Census Current Population Survey data to establish the representativeness of the sample to the population from which it was drawn. Initially it appeared that the sample over-represented the higher educational category. However, the actual differences are smaller than apparent differences when other factors are considered. The Census Current Population Survey data are based only on the education of persons 25 years old and over. There was thus a high degree of similarity between the sample distribution and the total population on demographic characteristics.

TABLE A.1.

SEX OF 1973 SAMPLE OF LEWISTON, IDAHO AND U.S. BUREAU OF CENSUS
1970 CURRENT POPULATION SURVEY

1973 Lewiston Sample						1970 Bureau of Census Population Survey[a]					
Male		Female		Total		Male		Female		Total	
N	%	N	%	N	%	N	%	N	%	N	%
111	(44.3)	139	(55.7)	249	(100)	8,084	(48.1)	8,745	(51.9)	16,829	(100)

[a]SOURCE: 1970 Census of Population. Characteristics of the Population. Idaho. Vol. 1, Part 14. January, 1973. U.S. Department of Commerce.

TABLE A.2.

AGE LEVEL OF 1973 SAMPLE OF LEWISTON, IDAHO AND U.S. BUREAU OF CENSUS 1970 CURRENT POPULATION SURVEY

Age	1973 Lewiston Sample		1970 Bureau of Census Population Survey	
	N	%	N	%
65 and Over	35	14.0	2,643	16.8
45-64	75	30.1	5,356	33.8
35-44	53	21.2	2,917	18.4
25-34	60	24.0	2,126	13.4
20-24	18	7.2	1,889	11.9
18-19	8	3.2	898	5.7
Total	249	100.0	15,829	100.0

TABLE A.3.

EDUCATIONAL LEVEL OF 1973 SAMPLE OF LEWISTON, IDAHO AND BUREAU OF CENSUS 1970 CURRENT POPULATION SURVEY

Educational Level	1973 Lewiston Sample		1970 Bureau of Census Population Survey[a]	
	N	%	N	%
College Graduate	56	22.4	1,534	11.7
Some College	63	25.3	1,940[b]	14.7
High School Grad.	85	34.1	5,151	39.1
Some High School	36	14.6	2,705[b]	20.5
Grade School	6	2.4	1,852	14.0
No Information	3	1.2	--	--
Total	249	100.0	12,182	100.0

[a] Based on males and females 25 years old and over
[b] 1-to-3 years

Median school years completed		12.3
Percent high school graduates	33.4	61.3

TABLE A.4.

INCOME LEVEL OF 1973 SAMPLE OF LEWISTON, IDAHO AND BUREAU
OF CENSUS 1970 CURRENT POPULATION SURVEY

Total Family Income	1973 Lewiston Sample		1970 Bureau of Census Population Survey[b]	
	N	%	N	%
$20,000 and Over	19	7.6		
15,000-19,999	37	14.9 (22.5)[a]	1,902[a]	22.2
12,000-14,999	49	19.7	1,395	16.3
10,000-11,999	40	16.0	1,266	14.7
8,000-9,999	28	11.3	1,094	12.8
6,000-7,999	14	5.6	1,192	13.9
Under $6,000	43	17.3	1,723	20.1
No Information	19	7.6	--	--
Total	249	100.0	8,572	100.0

[a] Includes incomes from $15,000-$49,999

[b] Median income $ 8,799
Percent earning $15,000 or more   13.2

TABLE A.5.

RESIDENCE OF 1973 LEWISTON, IDAHO SAMPLE AND U.S. BUREAU
OF CENSUS 1970 CURRENT POPULATION SURVEY

Residence	1973 Lewiston Sample		1970 Bureau of Census Population Survey[a]	
	N	%	N	%
Urban	198	84.3	26,068	85.0
Rural	49	15.7	4,308	15.0
Total	247	100.0	30,376	100.0

[a]Includes Nez Perce County

APPENDIX B

SUPPLEMENTARY TABLES

TABLE B.1.

MEANS AND STANDARD DEVIATIONS ON LEGAL DECRIMINALIZATION
OF PUBLIC ORDER CRIMES BY SEX
(N = 249)

	Male (N = 111)		Female (N = 138)	
	Mean	Std. Dev.	Mean	Std. Dev.
Abortion	14.7	3.2	14.4	3.2
Prostitution	2.6	0.8	2.3	1.0
Homosexuality	6.7	2.0	6.7	2.2
Narcotics	12.3	2.8	12.4	2.9
Summated (Master) Index	37.3	6.9	36.6	7.1

TABLE B.2.

MEANS AND STANDARD DEVIATIONS ON LEGAL DECRIMINALIZATION
OF PUBLIC ORDER CRIMES BY INCOME
(N = 249)

	(N)	Abortion		Prostitu-tion		Homo-sexuality		Narcotics		Master Index	
		X	Std.D.	X	Std.D.	X	Std.D.	X	Std.D.	X	Std.D.
$20,000-Over	(19)	16.1	2.2	2.5	0.9	7.2	1.8	11.9	2.5	39.3	5.2
15,000-19,999	(37)	15.2	2.7	2.4	1.0	7.2	2.0	12.5	3.4	38.3	7.0
12,000-14,999	(49)	14.4	3.4	2.3	0.8	6.5	2.0	12.4	2.9	36.5	6.6
10,000-11,999	(40)	14.0	3.3	2.4	1.0	6.7	2.0	12.5	2.2	35.9	6.2
8,000-9,999	(28)	14.7	3.1	2.6	0.9	7.0	1.9	12.6	2.6	37.8	7.0
6,000-7,999	(14)	15.0	2.8	2.9	0.6	7.1	2.0	14.2	3.2	40.2	7.1
Under $6,000	(43)	13.5	3.5	2.2	1.0	6.1	2.4	11.5	2.9	34.4	8.0
No Information	(19)										
Total	249										

MEANS AND STANDARD DEVIATIONS ON LEGAL DECRIMINALIZATION
OF PUBLIC ORDER CRIMES BY AGE
(N = 249)

	(N)	Abortion		Prostitu- tion		Homo- sexuality		Narcotics		Master Index	
		X	Std.D.	X	Std.D.	X	Std.D.	X	Std.D.	X	Std.D.
65 and Over	(34)	13.4	3.2	2.2	1.0	6.0	2.1	11.2	2.3	33.3	6.8
45-64	(75)	14.2	3.7	2.3	0.9	6.8	2.3	12.6	2.9	36.9	7.8
35-44	(53)	14.9	2.8	2.5	1.0	6.7	1.7	12.0	2.6	37.2	5.7
25-34	(60)	14.8	2.8	2.5	0.8	6.9	2.2	12.5	2.7	37.7	6.4
20-24	(18)	15.1	3.4	2.4	1.0	6.7	1.8	12.8	4.2	38.5	7.9
18-19	(8)	17.1	1.9	2.2	1.0	7.8	0.9	14.6	2.8	42.7	1.8
No Information	(1)										
Total	249										

TABLE B.4.

MEANS AND STANDARD DEVIATIONS ON LEGAL DECRIMINALIZATION
OF PUBLIC ORDER CRIMES BY EDUCATION
(N = 249)

	(N)	Abortion		Prostitu- tion		Homo- sexuality		Narcotics		Master Index	
		X	Std.D.	X	Std.D.	X	Std.D.	X	Std.D.	X	Std.D.
College Grad.	(56)	15.3	2.8	2.2	0.9	7.5	2.1	13.2	3.0	39.0	6.9
Some College	(62)	14.6	3.5	2.5	0.9	7.0	2.1	12.6	2.9	37.0	7.8
High School Grad.	(85)	14.3	3.0	2.5	0.9	6.2	2.0	11.9	2.5	36.2	6.1
Some High School	(36)	14.3	3.0	2.3	1.0	6.2	2.0	11.5	2.9	25.6	6.7
Grade School	(6)	11.0	4.3	2.1	1.3	6.0	1.5	11.3	2.0	31.3	8.7
No Information	(3)										
Total	249										

TABLE B.5.

MEANS AND STANDARD DEVIATIONS OF LEGAL DECRIMINALIZATION
OF PUBLIC ORDER CRIMES BY RELIGION
(N = 249)

	Protestants (N = 168)		Catholics (N = 36)		Mormon (N = 10)		Other (N = 25)	
	X	Std.D.	X	Std.D.	X	Std.D.	X	Std.D.
Abortion	14.8	3.0	13.5	3.7	12.2	2.2	15.4	3.4
Prostitution	2.4	0.9	2.4	1.0	1.8	1.0	2.8	1.0
Homosexuality	6.6	2.1	7.0	1.9	5.6	1.7	7.8	2.2
Narcotics	11.8	2.9	13.4	2.6	12.6	1.6	13.6	2.9
Summated Index	36.7	6.8	36.5	6.7	32.7	4.8	40.2	7.9

TABLE B.6

MEANS AND STANDARD DEVIATIONS ON THE PUNISHMENT
CONTINGENCY AND PUBLIC ORDER CRIMES BY SEX
(N = 249)

	Male		Female	
	Mean	Std.D.	Mean	Std.D.
Narcotics	4.8	2.1	4.2	2.2
Marijuana	6.5	2.3	6.2	2.3
Homosexuality	6.3	3.4	6.1	3.6
Summated Index	17.7	5.8	16.6	6.0

TABLE B.7.

MEANS AND STANDARD DEVIATIONS ON THE PUNISHMENT
CONTINGENCY AND PUBLIC ORDER CRIMES BY INCOME
(N = 249)

	(N)	Narcotics		Marijuana		Homo-sexuality		Master Index	
		X	Std.D.	X	Std.D.	X	Std.D.	X	Std.D.
$20,000-Over	(19)	4.7	1.8	7.0	1.1	6.9	3.9	18.7	4.5
15,000-19,999	(37)	5.0	2.3	6.7	2.2	7.4	3.2	19.2	5.1
12,000-14,999	(49)	4.6	2.3	5.6	2.6	5.3	3.5	15.6	6.3
10,000-11,999	(40)	4.5	1.8	6.3	2.1	6.1	3.7	16.9	6.0
8,000-9,999	(28)	3.7	2.3	6.4	2.5	6.5	3.4	16.6	6.0
6,000-7,9999	(14)	4.6	2.0	6.9	1.9	5.9	3.7	17.5	5.4
Under $6,000	(43)	4.3	2.5	6.4	2.4	6.1	3.3	17.0	6.5
No Information	(19)								
Total	249								

TABLE B.8.

MEANS AND STANDARD DEVIATIONS ON THE PUNISHMENT
CONTINGENCY AND PUBLIC ORDER CRIMES BY AGE
(N = 249)

	(N)	Narcotics		Marijuana		Homo-sexuality		Master Index	
		X	Std.D.	X	Std.D.	X	Std.D.	X	Std.D.
65 and Over	(34)	4.7	2.4	6.0	2.0	5.8	3.1	16.7	6.1
45-64	(75)	4.6	2.4	6.4	2.5	6.8	3.2	17.7	5.6
35-44	(53)	4.3	2.1	6.5	2.0	6.4	3.8	17.4	5.7
25-34	(60)	4.1	2.1	6.0	2.4	5.4	3.8	15.5	6.3
20-24	(18)	4.8	1.9	6.6	2.8	6.7	3.4	18.2	6.2
18-19	(8)	4.1	2.1	7.5	1.6	8.0	3.7	19.6	3.3
No Information	(1)								
Total	249								

TABLE B.9.

MEANS AND STANDARD DEVIATIONS ON THE PUNISHMENT CONTINGENCY AND PUBLIC ORDER CRIMES BY EDUCATION
(N = 249)

	(N)	Narcotics		Marijuana		Homo-sexuality		Master Index	
		X	Std.D.	X	Std.D.	X	Std.D.	X	Std.D.
College Grad.	(56)	4.5	2.5	6.8	2.5	6.6	3.5	18.0	6.0
Some College	(62)	4.5	2.1	6.3	2.5	6.2	3.9	16.9	6.3
High School Grad	(85)	4.4	2.1	6.2	2.1	5.9	3.4	16.6	5.8
Some High School	(36)	4.3	2.0	5.9	2.2	6.4	3.3	16.6	5.6
Grade School	(6)	7.1	0.4	6.8	2.2	7.6	1.2	21.6	2.6
No Information	(3)								
Total	249								

TABLE B.10.

MEANS AND STANDARD DEVIATIONS ON THE PUNISHMENT CONTINGENCY AND PUBLIC ORDER CRIMES BY RELIGION
(N = 249)

	Protestants (N = 168)		Catholics (N = 36)		Mormon (N = 10)		Other (N = 25)	
	X	Std.D.	X	Std.D.	X	Std.D.	X	Std.D.
Narcotics	4.3	2.2	5.0	2.2	4.0	1.4	4.9	2.5
Marijuana	6.2	2.1	6.1	2.7	4.9	2.3	7.4	2.6
Homosexuality	6.3	3.4	6.3	3.8	2.4	3.0	7.0	3.6
Summated Index	16.9	5.7	17.5	5.9	11.3	4.2	19.4	6.6

TABLE B.11.

MEANS AND STANDARD DEVIATIONS ON THE PUNISHMENT
CONTINGENCY AND PUBLIC ORDER CRIMES BY RESIDENCE
(N = 249)

	Urban (N = 198)		Rural (N = 49)	
	X	Std.D.	X	Std.D.
Narcotics	11.9	2.2	4.6	2.1
Marijuana	6.3	2.4	6.4	1.9
Homosexuality	6.4	3.5	5.7	3.6
Summated (Master) Index	17.2	5.9	16.7	5.9

TABLE B.12

MEANS AND STANDARD DEVIATIONS ON LEGAL DECRIMINALIZATION
OF PUBLIC ORDER CRIMES BY RESIDENCE
(N = 249)

	Urban (N = 198)		Rural (N = 49)	
	X	Std.D.	X	Std.D.
Abortion	14.6	3.2	14.1	3.4
Prostitution	2.5	0.9	2.1	0.8
Homosexuality	6.7	2.1	6.6	2.2
Narcotics	12.5	2.7	11.7	3.2
Summated (Master) Index	37.3	6.7	35.4	7.9

106

QUESTIONNAIRE SCHEDULE

STUDY ON LAW AND SOCIETY

The Sociology Department of the University of Idaho is conducting a research investigation of citizen's attitudes and opinions regarding crime and criminal laws. Very little is now known about the views of Idaho citizens regarding the handling of law-breakers and similar matters. As a result, the information that comes from the study should provide valuable facts for the legal profession, criminologists, and others as well. Your cooperation in this important investigation is earnestly requested. We do <u>not</u> want your name on the questionnaire, so that your responses will not be identified in any report that is made of the findings.

This questionnaire is relatively brief, so that it will not take very much of your time to complete.

This is a questionnaire to determine some of your attitudes toward crime, criminals and punishments. Many decisions have been made and judgements have been formed by the gathering of similar information from residents of California and other urban centers. We are extremely interested in the attitudes of the residents of Idaho. Your views and the time you spend to fill in this questionnaire will be greatly appreciated.

Below are a few questions regarding your background. These questions are asked in order that groups of people with similar backgrounds may be compared in the analysis of the information from this study. Your responses to these questions will be kept strictly confidential. Please check the appropriate spaces to the questions below. Thank you.

1. SEX

_____male

_____female

3. EDUCATION

_____college graduate

_____some college

_____high school graduate

_____some high school

_____grade school

2. AGE

_____over 65

_____45 to 65

_____35 to 44

_____25 to 34

_____20 to 24

_____under 20 years

4. RELIGION

_____Protestant _____Catholic

_____Jewish _____Mormon

_____Other

5. If Protestant, please list denomination

_____

6. Occupation of head of household

_____

7. Occupation of person filling out questionnaire, if other than 6

_____

8. Yearly income (of yourself and/or your spouse and family

_____over $20,000 _____$8-10,000

_____$15-20,000 _____$6-8,000

_____$10-12,000 _____under

$6,000

This is a questionnaire to determine some of your attitudes toward crime, criminals and punishments. Many decisions have been made and judgements have been formed by the gathering of similar information from residents of California and other urban centers. We are extremely interested in the attitudes of the residents of Idaho. Your views and the time you spend to fill in this questionnaire will be greatly appreciated.

Below are a few questions regarding your background. These questions are asked in order that groups of people with similar backgrounds may be compared in the analysis of the information from this study. Your responses to these questions will be kept strictly confidential. Please check the appropriate spaces to the questions below. Thank you.

1. SEX

_____male

_____female

3. EDUCATION

_____college graduate

_____some college

_____

2. AGE

_____over 65

_____45 to 65

_____35 to 44

_____25 to 34

_____20 to 24

_____under 20 years

9. <u>RESIDENCE BACKGROUND</u>

_____ Raised in Idaho and lived in Idaho   _____ Lived in Idaho for 10 years or more
        majority of life   _____ Lived in Idaho for 5 to 9 years
_____ Raised in rural area and lived in   _____ Lived in Idaho less than 5 years
        Idaho majority of life   _____ Lived in Idaho less than 5 years
_____ Raised in urban area and lived in   moved here from _____
        Idaho majority of life

I. <u>CRIME AND CRIMINAL POLICIES</u>

Listed below are statements about criminals, criminal laws, and similar matters.
Each of these is an argument or claim about which people have different opinions
and attitudes. Please check the category under each question which most closely
represents your opinion or attitude.

1. The police should be given greater powers to deal with criminals because as it now
   stands, criminals are too protected by laws of arrest, search and seizure and the
   like.

   _____   _____   _____   _____
   Strongly Agree   Agree   Disagree   Strongly Disagree

2. Most homosexuals are easy to 'spot' because of the way they dress, walk, talk, or
   due to their occupations.

   _____   _____   _____   _____
   Strongly Agree   Agree   Disagree   Strongly Disagree

3. Prostitution should be legalized and licensed so that prostitutes would be
   allowed to work at their trade in certain districts of the city.

   _____   _____   _____   _____
   Strongly Agree   Agree   Disagree   Strongly Disagree

4. It is a medical fact that in about one-third of the cases where a pregnant woman
   contacts German measles within the first 12 weeks of her pregnancy, various abnormalities result to the child. These include cataracts, deafness, microcephaly,
   and heart lesions. A pregnant woman who has German measles should be allowed to
   have an abortion, if she wishes one.

   _____   _____   _____   _____
   Strongly Agree   Agree   Disagree   Strongly Disagree

5. Homosexuals should be allowed to gather together in public places and to form
   organizations in order to obtain the civil rights which they are often denied
   under the present law.

   _____   _____   _____   _____
   Strongly Agree   Agree   Disagree   Strongly Disagree

6. It is probably true that the police arrest the majority of women who get illegal
   abortions, as well as the abortionists who commit the abortions.

   _____   _____   _____   _____
   Strongly Agree   Agree   Disagree   Strongly Disagree

7. Physicians and pharmacists who become drug addicts should have their licenses
   revoked and be heavily punished.

   _____   _____   _____   _____
   Strongly Agree   Agree   Disagree   Strongly Disagree

8. If two men in their 40's live together in a home that they have bought and furnished, there is good reason to suspect that they are homosexuals.

| Strongly Agree | Agree | Disagree | Strongly Disagree |

9. Since people in the medical professions have easy access to narcotics, there are, comparatively speaking, more drug addicts in these professions than in the general population.

| Strongly Agree | Agree | Disagree | Strongly Disagree |

10. Most homosexuals are neurotic and suffer from emotional disturbances. They should seek psychiatric help so that they may become adjusted to normal sexual relationships.

| Strongly Agree | Agree | Disagree | Strongly Disagree |

11. Most drug addicts are persons of weak character and are immoral.

| Strongly Agree | Agree | Disagree | Strongly Disagree |

12. Applications for abortions are sometimes made by women for psychiatric reasons. That is, they claim that their mental health or adjustment is threatened by their pregnancy. On occasion, these applications are supported by testimony of psychiatrists. The psychiatrist indicates that if the woman has the child, she may suffer serious psychological problems, including the possibility of suicide. Women who can show through expert psychiatric testimony that their psychological adjustment is seriously threatened by pregnancy should be allowed to have an abortion, if they wish one.

| Strongly Agree | Agree | Disagree | Strongly Disagree |

13. From time to time, recommendations have been made to the effect that the criminal laws against homosexual acts should be changed. If the laws were revised, acts of homosexual behavior between consenting adult partners would not be illegal. The laws should be so modified. Persons should be allowed to be homosexuals if they so desire.

| Strongly Agree | Agree | Disagree | Strongly Disagree |

14. Previous to the recent Supreme Court Decision, the existing abortion law in Idaho had allowed for therapeutic abortion (legal medical abortion) only in cases where it was necessary to save the life of the mother. In order to have had a legal abortion, it must have been shown that the pregnant woman was in extreme danger of dying before or during childbirth. This law should remain unchanged, so that abortion should not be allowed for any other reason.

| Strongly Agree | Agree | Disagree | Strongly Disagree |

15. Drug addiction is a sickness and should be dealt with as an illness rather than a crime.

| Strongly Agree | Agree | Disagree | Strongly Disagree |

16. Physicians should be allowed to treat narcotic addicts in the same way that they treat other sick persons. If a doctor thinks that an addict should be given some

drugs while the doctor tries to cure him of his addiction, the doctor should be allowed to carry out that form of treatment.

Strongly Agree   Agree   Disagree   Strongly Disagree

17. If all laws against homosexuality were done away with, this could become harmful to the welfare of society, in that homosexuals do not marry and do not produce children.

Strongly Agree   Agree   Disagree   Strongly Disagree

18. It is next to impossible for a drug addict to keep a legitimate job, since while he is under the influence of drugs he is unable to pay attention, to be alert, and so on.

Strongly Agree   Agree   Disagree   Strongly Disagree

19. There are many more homosexual males in Idaho than there are female homosexuals.

Strongly Agree   Agree   Disagree   Strongly Disagree

20. Both the non-addict peddler of drugs and the addict who peddles drugs (who sells drugs in order to support his habit) should be subjected to the same penalty under the law.

Strongly Agree   Agree   Disagree   Strongly Disagree

21. It is against the law in Idaho to engage in homosexual behavior--even voluntarily.

Strongly Agree   Agree   Disagree   Strongly Disagree

22. Alcoholism is a disease and alcoholics should be dealt with as 'sick' persons.

Strongly Agree   Agree   Disagree   Strongly Disagree

23. The laws in this country are usually made by men. However, we should pay more attention to the advice and opinion of women when drafting laws regarding abortion. After all, it is the women who have the children.

Strongly Agree   Agree   Disagree   Strongly Disagree

24. People who are using drugs such as marijuana usually are physical wrecks because the drugs are detrimental to a person's health.

Strongly Agree   Agree   Disagree   Strongly Disagree

25. Most abortions in the United States are performed upon young unmarried girls.

Strongly Agree   Agree   Disagree   Strongly Disagree

26. Homosexuality is immoral.

Strongly Agree   Agree   Disagree   Strongly Disagree

27. Most drug addicts are poverty-stricken and come from the slums.

Strongly Agree   Agree   Disagree   Strongly Disagree

28. People who smoke marijuana are more likely to commit various bad acts, including sex crimes, than are persons who don't use marijuana.

Strongly Agree   Agree   Disagree   Strongly Disagree

29. Adult homosexuals are dangerous, because they often try to recruit or seduce young boys into homosexual practices.

Strongly Agree   Agree   Disagree   Strongly Disagree

30. Existing narcotics laws in Idaho have the effect of making the use of opium, heroin, cocaine, and other opium derivatives for other than medical reasons illegal. These laws should be continued, and if anything they should be strengthened.

Strongly Agree   Agree   Disagree   Strongly Disagree

31. One thing to be said in favor of prostitution is that it keeps the number of sex crimes lower.

Strongly Agree   Agree   Disagree   Strongly Disagree

32. More programs for treating drug addicts organized along the lines of Synanon are needed in the United States.

Strongly Agree   Agree   Disagree   Strongly Disagree

33. Decreasing the penalties against crimes such as homosexuality, drug use, prostitution and abortion will lead to the downfall of the United States as it did with other great nations.

Strongly Agree   Agree   Disagree   Strongly Disagree

34. A homosexual would not be a desirable employee in government or industry because most likely the other employees would disapprove of having to work in the same office or area with him.

Strongly Agree   Agree   Disagree   Strongly Disagree

35. Marijuana should be legalized for adults, so that any adult who wanted to use it could purchase marijuana cigarettes in a store.

Strongly Agree   Agree   Disagree   Strongly Disagree

36. Females who have been raped sometimes get pregnant as a result, which is also true of girls who have been involved in incest with their fathers. Females who are pregnant due to rape or incest should be allowed to have an abortion, if they wish one.

Strongly Agree   Agree   Disagree   Strongly Disagree

37. The laws should be changed in the United States so as to make the use of alcohol in any form, including beer, against the law.

Strongly Agree   Agree   Disagree   Strongly Disagree

38. Very few criminal abortions in the United States are carried out by trained medical doctors.

Strongly Agree   Agree   Disagree   Strongly Disagree

39. Abortions should be illegal under all circumstances, including even those cases where the pregnant mother's life is in danger due to pregnancy.

Strongly Agree   Agree   Disagree   Strongly Disagree

40. Many of the sex crimes that occur in the United States are committed by persons who are drug addicts.

Strongly Agree   Agree   Disagree   Strongly Disagree

41. People who are under the influence of alcohol are more likely to commit crimes, including sex crimes, than people who have not been drinking.

Strongly Agree   Agree   Disagree   Strongly Disagree

II. EXPLANATORY STATEMENTS

On the next two pages, three different cases of criminal behavior are described. After you read one you are asked to indicate the sentence of punishment that you regard as most suitable or deserving in each case. The purpose of these questions is to find out what you think should be done with different criminal or delinquent persons.

Please pick out the penalty in each case which you regard as most appropriate for the offender described in that case. In the event you think something should be done with the person other than the sentences listed, write in your recommendation in the space marker "Other."

1. Bill Bishop is a 25-year old male who lives in a cheap hotel in the downtown area of city X. The police get a 'tip' that Bishop is a narcotics user. They manage to get into Bishop's hotel room where they surprise him in the act of flushing several capsules of heroin down the toilet. They also find a hypodermic needle below the window of his room. He is arrested and taken to court on charges of 'possession of narcotics.' His previous arrest record shows that he has been convicted of two instances of petty theft, but no previous drug charges. He is convicted of the narcotics charge in this instance.

   If you were in a position to decide the question, which of the sentences or dispositions below do you believe would be the most reasonable in this case? Check the appropriate sentence.

   _____Execution

   _____Prison sentence of over 10 years but less than 15 years

   _____Prison sentence of over 5 years but less than 10 years

   _____Prison sentence of over 1 year but less than 5 years

   _____Jail term of six months in length

   _____Jail term of one month in length

   _____Probation and supervision by a probation officer

   _____Fine of around $100 without jail or probation

   _____No penalty

   _____Other: _____

2. Stanley Stevens is a 26 year old homosexual. He admits that he is a homosexual and he associates frequently with other homosexual persons. One evening, he and a homosexual partner are surprised by the police as Stevens is performing a homosexual act on the other man. Both men are arrested and charged with the commission of lewd acts on the other man. Both Stevens and his partner in the crime are adults and they freely entered into the homosexual act. Stevens is convicted, as is his partner. Stevens has no record of any previous criminal actions.

   If you were in a position to decide the question, which of the sentences or dispositions below do you believe would be the most reasonable in this case? Check the appropriate sentence or disposition.

_____Execution

_____Prison sentence of over 10 years but less than 15 years

_____Prison sentence of over 5 years but less than 10 years

_____Prison sentence of over 1 year but less than 5 years

_____Jail term of six months in length

_____Jail term of one month in length

_____Probation and supervision by a probation officer

_____Fine of around $100 without jail or probation

_____No penalty

_____Other: _____

3. A group of local residents, including some college students, decide to have a 'pot' party, that is, a party at which they will smoke marijuana cigarettes. They arrange for the party at one of the group's apartments and obtain some marijuana. About an hour after the party has begun and they have all smoked some 'pot' (marijuana) a group of policemen appear at the apartment and arrest them. None of the marijuana smokers have previously been arrested, but all of them are convicted of the present charge.

If you were in a position to decide the question, which of the sentences or dispositions below do you believe would be the most reasonable in this case? Check the appropriate disposition or sentence.

_____Execution

_____Prison sentence of over 10 years but less than 15 years

_____Prison sentence of over 5 years but less than 10 years

_____Prison sentence of over 1 year but less than 5 years

_____Jail term of six months in length

_____Jail term of one month in length

_____Probation and supervision by a probation officer

_____Fine of around $100 without jail or probation

_____No penalty

_____Other: _____